Desano Grammar
Studies in the Languages of Colombia 6

Summer Institute of Linguistics and
The University of Texas at Arlington
Publications in Linguistics

Publication 132

Publications in Linguistics is a series published jointly by the Summer Institute of Linguistics and the University of Texas at Arlington. The series is a venue for works covering a broad range of topics in linguistics, especially the analytical treatment of minority languages from all parts of the world. While most volumes are authored by members of the Institute, suitable works by others will also form part of the series.

Series Editor
Donald A. Burquest
Summer Institute of Linguistics
University of Texas at Arlington

Volume Editors
Marilyn A. Mayers
Laurie Nelson

Production Staff
Margaret González, Compositor
Hazel Shorey, Graphic Artist

Desano Grammar
Studies in the Languages of Colombia 6

Marion Miller

A Publication of
The Summer Institute of Linguistics
and
The University of Texas at Arlington

©1999 by the Summer Institute of Linguistics, Inc.
Library of Congress Catalog No: 99-60307
ISBN: 1-55671-076-3
ISSN: 1040-0850

Printed in the United States of America
All Rights Reserved

09 08 07 06 05 04 03 02 01 00   10 9 8 7 6 5 4 3 2 1

No part of this publication may be reproduced, stored in a retrieval system, or transmitted in any form or by any means—electronic, mechanical, photocopy, recording, or otherwise—without the express permission of the Summer Institute of Linguistics, with the exception of brief excerpts in journal articles or reviews.

Copies of this and other publications of the Summer Institute of Linguistics may be obtained from

International Academic Bookstore
Summer Institute of Linguistics
7500 W. Camp Wisdom Rd.
Dallas, TX 75236-5699

Voice: 972-708-7404
Fax: 972-708-7433
Email: academic_books@sil.org
Internet: http://www.sil.org

Contents

Abbreviations ix

Acknowledgments xi

1. Introduction 1

   1.1–1.11 Constituent-order typology overview

   1.1. Constituent order in independent clauses 2
   1.2. Order of direct and indirect objects 2
   1.3. Adpositions 3
   1.4. Descriptive modifiers, numerals, and demonstratives . . 3
   1.5. Genitives 5
   1.6. Affixation and verb auxiliaries 5
   1.7. Relative clauses 6
   1.8. Comparatives 6
   1.9. Negation 7
   1.10. Questions 8
   1.11. Summary 8

   1.12–1.16 Phonology

   1.12. Phonemes 9
   1.13. Nasalization 13
   1.14. Syllable structure 15
   1.15. Stress and tone 15
   1.16. Morphophonemics 17

2. Parts of Speech		21
2.1.	Nouns	21
2.2.	Verbs	23
2.3.	Adverbs	27
2.4.	Pronouns	30
2.5.	Interjections	32
2.6.	Particles	34
3. Noun Phrase and Noun Phrase Operations		35
3.1.	Nouns	35
3.2.	Noun classifiers	35
3.3.	The article *dipa-*	44
3.4.	Quantifiers	44
3.5.	Numerals	46
3.6.	Diminutives and augmentatives	47
3.7.	Genitive constructions	48
3.8.	Descriptive modifiers	51
3.9.	Plurals	52
3.10.	Postpositions	54
3.11.	Limiters	55
4. Case		57
4.1.	The specific object marker *-re*	57
4.2.	Locative marker	59
4.3.	Instrument and accompaniment marker	62
5. Verb Phrase		63
5.1.	Agreement	64
5.2.	Tense-evidentials	64
5.3.	Tense markers	69
5.4.	Imperative	72
5.5.	Aspectuals	76
5.6.	Directionals	80
5.7.	Modal suffixes	81
5.8.	Miscellaneous suffixes	84
5.9.	Auxiliary verbs	87

Contents

5.10–5.12 Verb compounding

- 5.10. Bound verb roots that modify the main verb 90
- 5.11. Bound verb roots that function as a main verb 97
- 5.12. Independent verb roots that frequently occur in compounds 100
- 5.13. Noun incorporation 108
- 5.14. Denominalization 110

6. Valence Changing Operations 113
- 6.1. Valence increasing operations 113
- 6.2. Valence decreasing operations 118

7. Sentence Structure 123
- 7.1. Intransitive, transitive, and bitransitive clauses 123
- 7.2. Predicate nominals and predicate adjectives 125
- 7.3. Existential and predicate locative constructions 126
- 7.4. Possessive constructions 127

8. Question Formation 129
- 8.1. Polar questions 129
- 8.2. Information questions 131
- 8.3. Question particles 133

9. Negation 135
- 9.1. Standard clausal negation 135
- 9.2. Lexical negation 136
- 9.3. Constituent negation 137
- 9.4. Quantifier negation 137

10. Subordination 139

10.1–10.3 Nominalizations
- 10.1. Markers that deverbalize a verb 139
- 10.2. Types of nominalizations 142
- 10.3. Functions of nominalizations 144

10.4–10.7 Adverbial clauses
- 10.4. Time 150
- 10.5. Manner 151
- 10.6. Purpose 152

10.7.	Location	154
10.8.	Clause chaining and switch reference	154
11. Pragmatic Considerations		161

11.1–11.3 Pragmatic markers

11.1.	The contrastive -pɨ	161
11.2.	The additive -sã	163
11.3.	The limiters -ta and ta-bẽrã	163
11.4.	Pragmatic considerations affecting constituent order	166
11.5.	Introduction of participants	168
11.6.	Coherence devices	170
11.7.	Conjunctions	174
11.8.	Episodic prominence	175
References		177

Abbreviations

A	agent	LIM	limiter
ABIL	abilitative	LOC	locative
ABS	absolutely	m	masculine
AN	animate	MAN	manner
ASSUM	assumed evidential	MIGHT	future might
BEN	benefactive	MOVE	movement
CL	classifier	n	neuter
COMPLET	completive	NEG	negative
CONCES	concessive	NOM	nominalizer
CONTIN	continuative	NP	noun phrase
DESID	desiderative	P	patient
DIM	diminutive	p	plural
DIMIN	diminisher	PASS	passive
DVB	deverbalizer	PERF	perfective
f	feminine	PERT	pertaining to
FOC	focus	POT	potential
FRUST	frustrative	PRES	present
FUT	future	PROB	future probability
GEN	genitive	PST	past
HAB	habitual	Q	question marker
HORT	hortatory	RECIP	reciprocal
HSY	hearsay evidential	REC^PST	recent past
i	inclusive plural	REFL	reflexive
IMP	imperative	S	subject
INTEN	intensifier	s	singular

SING	singularizer	x	exclusive plural
SPC	specifier	1	first person
SR	switch reference	2	second person
TEL	telic	3	third person
TOTAL	totality	NON3	nonthird person
VB	verbalizer		

Acknowledgments

The study of language can be compared to an explorer mapping out new territory or a miner working a deep vein of gold. Desano is such a rich, interesting language that years could be spent digging up and revealing more nuggets, both about the grammar and the phonology. My husband and I have worked full-time with the Desano from 1963 to 1984 and part-time since that date. This grammar is an attempt to explain what has been discovered so far.

I would like to acknowledge the following people for their invaluable help without which this study would not have been completed.

The Desano people have patiently taught my husband and me their language and tried to explain some of the intricacies that we could not understand.

I am indebted to our colleagues who work in other Eastern Tucanoan languages for insights that they have passed on, either in discussion or in articles they have published. Although Jonathan Kaye started his Desano studies at the same time as the author, we each have made our observations independently of one another except for some informal sharing at the beginning. References to Kaye's 1970 dissertation are made throughout this volume.

As I began the formal write-up of the Desano grammar, I had the advantage of studying with Tom and Doris Payne and working through the *Field Manual for Descriptive Linguistics* written by Tom. Terry Malone did a careful study of the first draft giving many helpful suggestions.

Stephen Levinsohn not only gave to this grammar his linguistic expertise, but also his skills in clearly expressing information so that the reader can grasp the concepts. Thank you, Stephen.

1
Introduction

The Desano people[1] live in the southeastern part of Colombia in the department called the Vaupés and also across the border in Brazil. The majority live on tributaries of the main rivers, the Vaupés and the Papurí. Some have settled among other indigenous groups in larger communities along the Vaupés and Papurí rivers. In these communities the children generally grow up speaking the language of the dominant group rather than their own language. This is usually their mother's language since Desanos are not allowed to marry Desanos; rather, they marry cross-cousins or others from the neighboring indigenous groups who also belong linguistically to the Eastern Tucanoan language family (Waltz and Wheeler 1972:128). Those with Desano parentage (father) number around 1,000 people. Although many Desanos can speak Spanish with varying degrees of fluency, in their own villages they almost exclusively use their own language. Most small children and older adults know almost no Spanish, although they understand other Tucanoan languages because of cross marriages.

There are twenty-two Desano dialects. The names of the dialects are listed in the Desano-Spanish school dictionary (Miller, to appear). Each dialect represents a group called children of 'the name of the group'. The Desanos themselves have arranged the various groups into hierarchical order. The top group is *boreka porã* 'bass fish children', and the lowest group is *dĩhĩkẽrã* or *oyoa* 'servants'. In the middle of this hierarchy is a subgroup called *si?bia bãsã*. In this subgroup there are three dialect groups. They live in Brazil, and the Desanos of the other groups say that their dialects are mutually unintelligible with the rest of the

---

[1] The Desano people use the form *wĩrã* for their language and language family. The origin of this term is not known. They use *wĩrã* when referring to themselves in Desano, but call themselves Desano in Spanish.

groups. The top groups are said to be the older brother of the others, and the lower groups are called 'our grandparents'. We have made comparisons among four groups, and the greatest differences have been noted between the *boreka porã* 'bass fish children' and the *sūbūperu porã* 'type of fish children' dialects. The main difference is noted in the sentence introducer word 'thus' that is very commonly used. In the former dialect it is *eropa* and in the latter *daha*. Examples in this grammar are from the *boreka porã* dialect, as is the material in Kaye's thesis.

The following is a typological summary of Desano which shows that Desano has most of the correlates of an SOV language.

1.1–1.11 Constituent-order typology overview

1.1. Constituent order in independent clauses

A text study of 150 Desano independent clauses in continuous text, with their accompanying dependent clauses, shows that the basic constituent order in Desano is OV with the subject (S) generally preceding the verb (V) and the object/patient (O). The following table shows the distribution of subject, object, and verb in the independent declarative transitive, including bitransitive clauses. Desano is a nominative-accusative language (§7.1).

(1) Distribution of S, O, and V in transitive clauses

OV	VO	SV	VS
34	8	11	6

The preferred clause structure in long narratives is verb plus one or no overtly expressed arguments. On a count of 150 clauses, only 23 contained the verb plus two arguments. This is not the pattern in more isolated sentences where the subject and object both need to be identified. In a letter written by a Desano covering various topics, 9 out of 11 transitive clauses had both the subject and object overtly expressed with a noun, clause, or pronoun.

1.2. Order of direct and indirect objects

The order of direct and indirect objects, when both occur in the clause, is flexible, though both generally precede the verb. The direct object takes either no marker or *-re,* which is a specifier (see §4.1). The

Introduction

indirect object obligatorily takes *-re*. Examples of direct and indirect objects in a clause are given in (2)–(3).

(2) *erop-ii-gɨ   iri-re   bɨ̃ã-re   were-dia-bɨ*
     thus-do-ms this-SPC 2p-SPC say-DESID-NON3^PST
     Therefore, I wanted to advise you of this.

(3) *Lino bɨ̃ã-re   i   kere   obeo-a-bɨ̃*
     Lino 2p-SPC this news send-REC^PST-3ms
     Lino sent the following message to you.

1.3 Adpositions

Desano uses only postpositions in adpositional phrases. Examples (4)–(6) illustrate postpositions (see also §3.10).

(4) *gūbūri doka*
     logs   below
     under logs

(5) *yukɨgɨ gobe poʔeka-ge*
     tree   hole inside-LOC
     inside a hole in a tree

(6) *goe-ri   bohe kore*
     return-DVB time before
     before noon

1.4. Descriptive modifiers, numerals, and demonstratives

The DESCRIPTIVE MODIFIER, described in §3.8, generally precedes the head noun in the noun phrase. When it goes before the head, it is marked with a deverbalizer but not with a class or gender marker. It follows the head noun when a demonstrative, number, or genitive precedes the noun. Following the noun, the deverbalized modifier is inflected with the noun class or gender marker, or the noun is repeated if it does not have a separate class marker. Since, when the modifier follows the head noun, it has to take the noun class or gender marker, or the noun itself has to be repeated, it could be argued that in these cases the modifier is still preceding the head noun because it is preceding its substitute (see further discussion in §10.1–10.3).

Examples (7)–(10) show various occurrences of descriptive modifiers. Note that the modifiers in examples (8) and (10) occur following the head noun because a number precedes it; (10) is an illustration of a noun that is not classified so the noun is repeated after the deverbalized modifier. An alternative analysis is that the noun phrase occurs twice, in apposition, and in each instance the deverbalized modifier precedes the noun. In (8), however, only the classifier follows the modifier.

(7) yẽ-ri   diu-ri
    beˆbad-DVB egg-p
    bad eggs

(8) yuhu-ru wɨ-ri-ru   wɨa-ri-ru
    one-CL   fly-DVB-CL large-DVB-CL
    one large plane

(9) baha-rã   bãsã
    aˆlot-AN   people
    many people

(10) yuhu gobe ĩʔkã-ri   gobe
     one hole deep-DVB hole
     a deep hole

NUMERALS usually occur before the head noun, or follow the head noun and precede the classifier. They follow the demonstrative when it is in the same noun phrase. With animate nouns, the numerals often follow the head noun; the numerals carry the gender or class suffix that agrees with the noun.

(11) ɨʔre   wiʔi
     three   house
     three houses

(12) suʔri   pe-yẽ   opa-a
     clothes two-CL   have-NON3ˆPRES
     I have two dresses.

(13) ĩgɨ   porã   pe-rã
     3ms   children two-ANp
     his two children

Introduction

The DEMONSTRATIVES *i* (this), *si* (that), and *iri* (anaphoric) occur preceding the head noun and before the numeral in the noun phrase. They take a noun classifier when preceding or replacing inanimate, countable nouns. They can and most frequently do occur without the noun.

(14)   *i*   *bõʔbẽ-ri*
       this   work-DVB
       this work

(15)   *iri*   *wapikɨ-ri sebãdã*
       this   four-DVB   week
       these four weeks

(16)   *iri-ru-re*   *kore-rã*
       this-CL-SPC   wait-ANp
       waiting for this (plane)

1.5. Genitives

In a possessive phrase, the genitive *ya* precedes the head noun as in (17)–(18); *ya* can occur alone without a head noun when referring to nonindividuated inanimate objects as in (19). See §3.7 for further discussion of the genitive.

(17)   *gɨa ya*   *wiʔi*
       1x   GEN   house
       our house

(18)   *yɨʔɨ-ya*[2] *bãleta*
       1s-GEN   suitcase
       my suitcase

(19)   *igo ya*
       3fs   GEN
       her things

1.6. Affixation and verb auxiliaries

Affixation in Desano consists of suffixes only. The verb morphology of the language is quite extensive with suffixes expressing emphasis,

---

[2] *yɨʔɨ-ya* is contracted to *yaʔa* in normal speech.

direction of movement, causation, benefaction, negation, contra-expectation, as well as evidentiality, aspect, tense-mood, and person-number. Verbs may also take derivational suffixes to form nouns or adverbs, including descriptive modifiers which are formed in the same way as nouns. Example (20) shows a nominalized verb with a root and four suffixes and also illustrates the use of the auxiliary *ii-* 'do', which is one of the ways in Desano to code causation (§6.1).

(20) ẽrã gɨa bãsĩ-biri-bo-ra-re   bãsĩ-kɨ   ii-bã
     3p   1x   know-NEG-POT-DVB-SPC know-SR   do-3p
     They caused us to know what we didn't know but/and had potential for knowing.

The auxiliary verbs in Desano are *ii-* 'do' and *wa-* 'go' (see §5.9). They follow the main verb that carries the semantic load.

(21) bõhõtõ yẽã   ii-bã   gɨa-re
     hand   grasp do-3p   1x-SPC
     They shook our hand.

(22) kãrĩ-a   wa-bĩ
     sleep-PERF   go-3ms
     He has fallen asleep.

1.7. Relative clauses

Relative clauses in Desano follow the head noun. The verbs in these clauses are always nominalized and agree with the head noun (see §10.1). They can take the same inflectional suffixes as the main verb, except for evidentiality markers, but for semantic reasons they tend to be more restricted. In example (23) the relative clause is bracketed.

(23) Alfonso [gahi-gɨ   ari-dia-di-gɨ]
     Alfonso other-ms   come-DESID-PST-ms
     Alfonso, the other one who wanted to come

1.8. Comparatives

In comparative constructions, the comparative postposition *dopa*, often followed by the limiter *-ta* (§11.3), follows the standard of comparison. Comparative constructions can be a word, a clause, or a phrase.

(24) *pera dopa-ta ã?rĩ-bã*
pera like-LIM be-3p
They are like the *pera* (a large ant with a painful sting).

(25) *bĩã yɨ-re õã-ro ii-ro dopa-ta yɨ-sã bĩã bẽrã*
2p 1s-SPC beˆgood-DVB do-DVB like-LIM 1s-also 2p with

 õã-ro árĩ-dia-a
 beˆgood-DVB be-DESID-NON3ˆPRES
 I want to be well with you like you do well to me.

1.9. Negation

Standard negation is accomplished in Desano by the suffix *-biri* which, with its variants *-bi* and *-bea*, occurs with all verb forms; *-bi/-bẽ* also negativizes the quantifier *baha-* 'a lot'. There is also a negative future suffix *-sobẽ* 'will not do' which occurs verb final, and there are two negative verbs: *bãrĩ-* 'not be' and *bõõ-* 'not have' (see chapter 9).

(26) *yɨ?ɨ bẽrã wa-dia-biri-ku-ri*
1s with go-DESID-NEG-ASSUM-Q
Don't you want to go with me?

(27) *gɨa-re gahi-ro-pa ii-bãsĩ-biri-bã*
1x-SPC other-n-MAN do-ABIL-NEG-3p
They could not do otherwise to us.

(28) *bõ?bẽ-bi-gɨ ã?rĩ-bĩ*
work-NEG-ms be-3ms
He is a non-worker.

(29) *wai baha-bẽ-rã wẽhẽ-bã*
fish aˆlot-NEG-ANp kill-3p
They killed a few fish.

(30) *deko bẽrẽ-sobẽ*
water fall-NEGˆFUT
It will not rain.

(31) *a?ɨ-sã bãrĩ-di-rã árĩ-bã*
father-also notˆbe-PST-ANp be-3p
My parents weren't there.

(32) dẽ   yõkã   bārī bõõ-a
     first manioc^drink 1i   not^have-NON3^PRES
     We don't have any manioc drink at all.

1.10. Questions

In polar questions (§8.1), the question marker is a suffix that occurs at the end of the main verb and replaces the person, number, and gender suffixes that would have occurred there.

(33) biaporã wẽhẽ-ri-re   o-beo-biri-bo-ku-ri
     ants   kill-DVB-SPC give-send-NEG-POT-ASSUM-Q
     You wouldn't send out some ant-poison, would you?

(34) bɨã a?ra-ri
     2p come-Q
     Did you come?

In information questions (§8.2), the interrogative pronouns generally occur initially in the sentence while the question marker still appears on the verb.

(35) dõã dɨkɨ a?ra-ri
     who each come-Q
     How many came/Who all came?

(36) dipẽ   waha-kɨ-ri
     how^much pay-VB-Q
     How much does it cost?

Desano has a question particle, *ka*, that follows a noun or phrase to ask a question about the expression.

(37) bɨã porã   ka
     2s children Q
     What about your children?

1.11. Summary

A review of this section shows that Desano generally fits the pattern for OV languages. It is a suffixing language. There are only postpositions (no prepositions). Auxiliary verbs follow the main verb. Question words

Introduction

are sentence initial. Noun phrases have some variations: the genitive and the demonstrative modifiers precede the head, but the numerals and descriptive modifiers can both precede and follow the head noun, although they always precede either the head noun or its corresponding classifier. The relative clause also follows the head noun. In comparative constructions, the descriptive modifier follows the standard of comparison.

1.12–1.16 Phonology

1.12. Phonemes

Desano has eighteen phonemes: twelve consonants and six vowels. These are presented in (38)–(39).[3]

(38) Consonant phonemes

	labial	alveolar	velar	glottal
stop				
voiceless	p	t	k	ʔ
voiced	b	d	g	
fricative		s		h
flap		r		
semivowel	w	y		

(39) Vowel phonemes

	front	mid	back
high	i	ɨ	u
low	e	a	o

The phonemes are represented in this volume as they appear in the tables in (38)–(39). Nasalization, which is a suprasegmental feature of the morpheme (see §1.13) is indicated with a tilde above the vowels affected. Stress is also phonemic but is not written in this paper, except where it is needed to distinguish meaning.

For easier reading of examples, morphemes are represented in their underlying form. Under certain conditions, there is nasal spreading or

---

[3] For further information on studies of Desano phonology see Kaye (1970, 1971), Miller (1976).

vowel deletion that changes the surface form slightly. This is not normally shown, in order to keep a single form for each morpheme.

Kaye (1970:18) was unable to decide whether glottalized syllables were phonemic or were a function of accent. There are enough minimal pairs, however, to indicate that a glottalized sound is indeed a phoneme, even though some syllables change from stressed vowel to vowel followed by a glottal according to the placement of stress and high tone in the word. See §1.15. Example (40) lists syllables which always have a glottal stop contrasted with syllables that never have a glottal. The stress is the same in each of the contrastive pairs.

(40) guʔabõ   'she bathes'   guabõ   'she is angry'
     doʔpa   'yet'   dopa   'like'
     buʔriri   'does it jump?'   bɨriri 'is it hard?'

The phonemes /r/ and /d/ contrast only word medially in suffix initial positions (e.g., pe-ru 'two canoes', pe-da 'two strings'); /r/ does not begin a word, while /d/ is never found in the middle of a morpheme. Furthermore, in the case of some suffixes, some dialects use /r/ while others use /d/. For example, the past form of the participle is -ra in some dialects and -da in others. This is probably why Kaye (1970:14) treats [ɾ] as an allophone of /d/. Nevertheless, there is no rule that predicts when to use /d/ and when to use /r/ suffix initially. Consequently, /d/ and /r/ are treated as separate phonemes in this volume.[4]

Contrasts between consonant phonemes are shown in (41). Variations of the consonant phonemes are then described and illustrated in (42)–(45).

(41) p/b/w   paʔa-   'crawl'
              baʔa-   'eat'
              waʔa-   'go'

     t/d   tea-   'pick fruit'
              dea-   'mash'

     y/d   yaji   'egret'
              daji   'thus' (sūbūperu porã dialect)

---

[4] Malone (1991) proposes for Proto-Tucanoan a phoneme /*d/ with allophones [d], [ɾ], [n], [r], [flap n].

Introduction

d/r/s	ba-di-gɨ	'the one who ate'
	ba-ri-kɨ-bĩ	'he has food'
	basi	'himself'
k/g	kuiri	'eyes'
	gui-ri	'fear'
ʔ/h	oho	'banana'
	oʔo-	'give'

The consonants /b/, /d/, /g/ and the semivowels /y/, /w/, /h/ have nasal variants at the same point of articulation when they occur in a nasal morpheme, as shown in (42). The phonetic representation is enclosed in square brackets.

(42)
	b	[mõhõa]	/bõhõa/	'it dries'
		[bohoɾi]	/bohori/	'year'
	d	[nõã]	/dõã/	'who'
		[doa-]	/doa-/	'sit'
	g	[ŋõãɾĩ]	/gõãrĩ/	'bones'
		[guaɾi]	/guari/	'are you angry?'
	y	[õñũ]	/õyũ/	'avocado'
		[oyo]	/oyo/	'bat'
	w	[w̃ẽh̃ẽ-]	/wẽhẽ-/	'kill'
		[wɛko]	/weko/	'parrot'
	h	[ẽh̃õ]	/ẽhõ/	'flu'
		[eho-]	/eho-/	'feed'

The alveolar flap /r/ has four variants. The vibrant [ɾ] and its nasal counterpart in nasal morphemes follow front vowels; the lateral approximant [l] and its nasal counterpart follow back vowels as in (43).

(43)
/r/	[ɾ]	[peɾu]	/peru/	'two canoes'
	[ɾ̃]	[peɾ̃ã]	/perã/	'two people'
	[l]	[aʔlaa]	/aʔraa/	'I come'
	[l̃]	[ãʔl̃ãã]	/ãʔrãã/	'I am'

The voiced stops that occur in syllables that are intrinsically nonnasal (see §1.13) are prenasalized when they appear word initially or follow a nasal morpheme.

(44) b [mbia]   /bia/   'hot pepper'
       [bãsĩmbirika] /bãsĩbirika/ 'I don't know'

     d [ndia]   /dia/   'river'
       [kãndihia]   /kãdihia/   'I forget'

     g [ŋgasiro]   /gasiro/   'bark'
       [sõʔõŋge]   /sõʔõge/   'there'

The glottal fricative /h/ and glottal stop /ʔ/ occur only intervocalically. They are followed by the echo of the vowel that precedes them.

(45) h [yahai]   /yahi/   'egret'
       [yãh̃ããbĩ]   /yãhãbĩ/   'he enters'

     ʔ [pɨʔɨlɨ]   /pɨʔrɨ/   'after'
       [oʔoake]   /oʔake/   'sweep'

There is some variation between speakers in the pronunciation of /y/ and /w/. Some speakers pronounce /y/ with friction, more like a [dz], and some vary /w/ between [w] and [v].

Contrasts between vowel phonemes are shown in (46) followed by a discussion of the vowel variations.

(46) i/e /wiribĩ/ 'he saws'   /werebĩ/ 'he speaks'
     i/ɨ /siabɨ/   'it hung'   /sɨabɨ/   'I liked (it)'
     ɨ/u /bɨpɨ/   'spider'   /bupu/   'thunder'
     u/o /duake/   'sell'   /doake/   'sit down'
     ɨ/a /bɨʔɨ̃/   'you'   /bãʔã/   'trail'

Apart from the nasal variants found in nasal morphemes, the following vowel variations occur.

The vowel /e/ varies between [e], close mid front, and [ɛ], open mid front, in certain words, e.g., [yɛse] /yese/ 'pig'; the conditioning is unknown.

If the middle consonant in the sequence (C)VCV is voiceless, the vowel that precedes it acquires a voiceless lengthening as in (47).

Introduction

(47) [dɛɛ̥'ko]   /dekó/   'water'
    [ãą̃'sũ]   /ãsṹ/   'buy'

Although /o/ and /u/ contrast in some intrinsically nasal morphemes such as gõã 'bone' and gũbũ 'log', there are certain words where there is free variation between the two, as in (48).

(48) [būyū] ~ [bõyõ]   'tobacco'
    [ũʔrã] ~ [õʔrã]   'howler monkey'

1.13. Nasalization

As in most of the other Tucanoan languages (see Bivin 1986:27), nasalization in Desano is a property of the morpheme since the vowels of any given morpheme are either all nasal or all oral, while most consonant variants are determined by whether the morpheme is intrinsically nasal or oral. All root morphemes are intrinsically nasal or oral. Suffixes can be instrinsically oral, instrinsically nasal, or can be termed 'chameleons' unspecified for nasality, i.e., either oral or nasal depending on environment (Jones and Jones 1991:14). Nasalization does not spread through an intrinsically oral suffix, thus an intrinsically oral suffix following a nasal morpheme stops the spread of nasalization through the word. The suffixes unspecified for nasality are made nasal by nasalization spreading to the right. This nasal assimilation occurs within the phonological word. Barnes's description of nasalization in Tuyuca (1996:32–40) would generally fit Desano, as well.

For example, the suffix -gɨ (masculine singular) is unspecified for nasality. When it follows an intrinsically oral root it is oral. When it follows an intrinsically nasal root it is nasal, for example, arigɨ 'if he comes', ãrĩgɨ̃ 'if he says'.

If -gɨ follows an intrinsically oral suffix, it is oral, even if the preceding root is nasal. If it follows an intrinsically nasal suffix or an unspecified suffix made nasal by the preceding stem or suffix, it is nasal.

(49) bāsīdiagɨ   'if he wants to know'
    bāsīdēbōgɨ̃   'if he knows more'
    bāsīãgɨ̃   'if he completely knows'

Some of the other suffixes that are unspecified for nasality are given in (50).

(50) -bu (classifier)   wehabu   'paddle'   ɨtābū   'rapids'
      -re (specifier)   igore   'to her'   bārīrē   'to us'
      -ya 'river   poyaya   'slave river'   dībāyā   'poison river'
           (classifier)'

Some of the intrinsically oral morphemes in Desano that resist nasal assimilation are given in (51).

(51) -bo (potential)   bāsībogɨ 'the one (ms) about to know'
      -ra (past deverbalizer)   bāsīra   'what was known'
      -di (past nominalizer)   bāsīdigɨ 'the one who knew'

Some examples of intrinsically nasal morphemes are listed in (52).

(52) -kã 'absolutely'   bāsīkābĩ 'he certainly knows'
                                   bakābĩ   'he certainly ate'

      -gã (diminutive)   bīgɨgã   'little one (ms)'
                                   wiʔigã   'little house'

As can be seen by the illustrations above, there is no grammatical or phonological pattern by means of which one can predict whether a morpheme will be inherently nasal, oral, or unspecified for nasality. This feature must be marked in the lexicon.

Desano has an additional feature of nasal assimilation that Bivin (1986:72) finds in only one other Tucanoan language, Siriano. Barasano (Jones and Jones 1991:16) has this feature on a more limited scale, i.e., certain suffixes acquire specification for nasality from four nasal suffixes on their right that define person and number on the word. The suffixes which accept nasal assimilation in this case are nevertheless considered inherently oral because they block nasal spread from the left.

With the intrinsically nasal suffix -rã (animate plural), a few suffixes that occur to its left become nasal. The examples in (53) also show these same suffixes blocking nasalization from the left.

(53) -bi (negative)   wẽhẽbīrã 'the ones who don't kill'
                                   wẽhẽbigɨ 'the one who doesn't kill'

      -di (past nominalizer)   wẽhẽdīrã 'the ones who killed'
                                   wẽhẽdigɨ 'the one who killed'

Introduction

-bo	(potential)	wẽhẽbõrã	'the ones about to kill'
		wẽhẽbogɨ	'the one about to kill'
-yu/-yo	(second-hand information)	wẽhẽyõrã	'they killed (reported)'
		wẽhẽyoro	'you killed (reported)'

The verb-final suffixes which indicate person and number for the subject (-bĩ (3ms), -bõ (3f), -bã (3p)) are inherently nasal and cause nasal spreading to a few suffixes on the left. The morphemes which the above suffixes affect are -ku/k (assumed present) and -yu/yo/y (assumed past). The examples in (54) again show the suffixes accepting nasal assimilation from the right and blocking it from the left.

(54) āsūkūbĩ 'he probably buys'   āsūka 'you probably buy'
     āsūyūbã 'they probably bought'   āsūyoro 'you probably bought'

Both in his dissertation (Kaye 1970) and in his *Linguistic Inquiry* article (Kaye 1971), Kaye tries to handle left-to-right and right-to-left nasal spread within one series of rules. Left-to-right spread is productive synchronically in Desano, whereas right-to-left is limited to only a few morphemes, and these morphemes are inherently oral. Given this distribution it seems appropriate to consider right-to-left nasal assimilation to be totally lexicalized.

1.14. Syllable structure

The most common syllable pattern is CV. The others are CV?, V, and V?. In (55), the syllable boundaries are separated by a period.

(55) CV   ga   'eagle'
     CV?.V   gu?.a-   'bathe'
     V.V   e.a   'sew'
     V?.CV.CV   a?.ri.bĩ   'he comes'

1.15. Stress and tone

The phonological word in Desano is composed of one to five syllables with one principal stress. The stressed syllable has high pitch. All others have low or mid pitch. Each root in the language carries its own basic stress/accent pattern. Verb roots, which typically have one or two syllables, can be classified into three different classes according to their pattern of pitch. This pattern is determined by conjugating the verb root with the suffix -*ke* (imperative), as example (56) shows.

(56) class 1 *séake* 'Dig!'
     class 2 *seáke* 'Cut hair!'
     class 3 *seaké* 'Gather!'

As can be seen in (56), the pattern of the first verb root class is stress on the first syllable. In the second it is stress on the second syllable, and on the third no stress.[5]

The accent pattern of a suffixed verb is predictable from the verb class of the root. For example, the three classes are conjugated with future and the assumed past evidential as in (57).

(57)
	root	future	assumed past evidential
class 1	*séa* 'dig'	*séagɨkubĩ*	*séayũbĩ*
class 2	*seá* 'cut hair'	*seágɨkubĩ*	*seáyũbĩ*
class 3	*sea* 'gather'	*seagɨkubĩ*	*seayũbĩ́*

When other morphemes are attached to these roots, however, the stress pattern is changed. For example, if another morpheme takes the stress in the word, then a class 1 root is no longer stressed on the first syllable and adds a glottal stop, as in *seʔabĩ́* 'he digs'.

Like verb stems, noun roots carry their own stress pattern, but there is more variety in the number of syllables. Some nouns with syllable

---

[5] Kaye mistakenly claimed that all verb roots in Desano are accented on their final syllable (1970:20). Janet Barnes (1996:40–58) suggests that in Tuyuca there are three accent categories on stems and suffixes: those marked with an associated accent, that is, they always carry the stress in the word except under some limited conditions; those marked with an unassociated accent which may or may not carry the stress in the word; and those that are unmarked and never receive word stress. In Desano, verb and noun roots that have stress on the first vowel could be said to be marked with an associated accent, since, even when they do not carry the accent in the word, they add a glottal stop. A few suffixes, such as -*yu* (second-hand information), could be classified as unmarked, since they never receive word stress. However, the vast majority of roots and suffixes would need to be classified as marked with unassociated accent, because the position of the accent is affected by the different suffixes and roots that may be added. It would therefore be unproductive to analyze Desano in the way that Barnes suggests for Tuyuca.

Introduction

pattern CVV́, such as wiʔí 'house', shorten to CV́ when followed by -re and certain other morphemes, though not with all suffixes.⁶

(58) wiʔí   'house'   wí-ri   'houses'
     wí-re   'in the house' wiʔi-gé   'at the house'

1.16. Morphophonemics

The kinds of morphophonemics which operate in Desano are vowel suppression, syllable reduction, and vowel harmony. Each of these are illustrated in the following discussion.

Various verb roots and suffixes ending with or consisting of the syllable *ri* lose the *i* when the vowel *a* follows. For a fuller discussion of such vowel suppression, which Kaye calls vowel coalescence, see Kaye 1970:180–86.⁷ Note examples of vowel suppression in (59)–(61).

(59) kārī +ri + a + bī becomes kārīrabī
     sleep-FRUST-RECˆPST-3ms
     He slept (not well).

(60) ba + biri + a + bī becomes babirabī
     eat-NEG-RECˆPST-3ms
     He did not eat.

(61) aʔri + a becomes aʔra with length on the final a
     come-NON3ˆPRES
     I come.

Syllable reduction results in various contracted forms in Desano. For example, the sequence *agɨ* is often contracted to *ɨ* as in (62). Some

---

⁶Over the years the glottal stop has been lost and replaced with only high pitch on some noun roots. The word waʔí 'fish' is rendered wáí by the younger people of the boreka dialect. These changes are on nouns and verbs that sometimes carry stress on the first syllable and sometimes lose the stress and add a glottal stop. On the nouns and verbs where the glottal stop stays in place no matter which suffixes are added, no change has been observed. An example of this kind of noun is ūʔrā 'howler monkey', ūʔrā-re 'to the howler monkey', and of a verb is guʔa- 'bathe', guʔake 'bathe!'.

⁷Kaye (1970:188–91) postulates that there is a "putative epenthetic vowel /ɑ/ that occurs on all verbs that do not end in a personal ending or question marker, after all pronouns, and on at least one noun final." Studies for this paper indicate that the *a* that occurs on the verb is a non-third person present marker (see §5.2); *a* is also a plural marker on animate nouns (§2.1.), while three of the four plural pronouns also end in *a* (§2.4). That leaves a tiny number of examples of word final *a* unaccounted for.

speakers delete the *gɨ* in the sequence *-digɨ* (past masculine singular). Other examples of syllable reduction are noted in later chapters.

(62)   *pagɨ*   'father'   becomes   *pɨ*
      wagɨra   'I will go'   becomes   *wɨra*

Some dialectical differences illustrate syllable reduction and variation between *d* and *r*. For the hearsay evidential, the *boreka* dialect deletes the *-yu* syllable whereas the others leave it in, as in (63). In three dialects there is a difference in the classifier of a canoe-shaped object as shown in (64). The past form of the participle *-ri* is *-ra* in dialect 1, example (65), but *-da* in other dialects.

(63)   Dialect 1 *boreka porã*   Other dialects
      wa-pɨ   *wa-yupɨ*
      go-HSY^3ms   go-HSY^3ms
      He went.

      wa-po   *wa-yupo*
      go-HSY^3fs   go-HSY^3fs
      She went.

      wa-yõrã   *wa-yõrã*
      go-HSY^3p   go-HSY^3p
      They went.

(64)   Dialect 1   Dialect 2   Dialect 3
      wɨ-di-ru   *wɨ-du*   *wɨ-ri-ru*
      fly-DVB-CL   fly-CL   fly-DVB-CL
      airplane

(65)   *goha-ri-a* becomes *goha-ra* or *goha-da*
      write-DVB-PST
      that which was written

In the *boreka* dialect, two classifiers show syllable reduction. The classifier *pa-yẽ* becomes *-pẽ*, and *-dõhõ* becomes *-dõ* (see §3.2).

Vowel harmony, involving vowel lowering, affects a limited number of verb suffixes (Kaye 1970:186–88): *-di-* (past nominative) changes to *-de-*, *-bi-* (negative) goes to *-be-*, *-bu-* (potential marker) becomes *-bo-*, *-ku-* (inferred evidential) goes to *-ko-*, and *-yu-* (inferred-hearsay

Introduction

evidential) becomes -yo-, as in (66).[8] Some speakers make the change and some do not.

(66) /wa-di-gɨ/   'the one (m) who went'
      /wa-di-go/ or /wadego/ 'the one (f) who went'
      /wa-dĩ-rã/ or /wadẽrã/ 'the ones who went'
      /wabugɨ/   'the one (m) about to go'
      /wabogo/   'the one (f) about to go'
      /waburi/   'being about to go'
      /wayũbĩ/   'he went (inferred)'
      /wayõbã/   'they went (inferred)'
      /wayoro/   'it didn't go'
      /wakũbĩ/   'he goes (inferred)'
      /wakõbõ/   'she goes (inferred)'
      /wabigɨ/   'the one (m) who doesn't go'
      /wabigo/   'the one (f) who doesn't go'
      /wabirã/ or /wabẽrã/   'the ones who don't go'
      /wabiribĩ/   'he didn't go'
      /wabeabĩ/   'he doesn't go'

---

[8] Kaye does not mention -*di* and -*bi*.

2
Parts of Speech

The major parts of speech in Desano are nouns, verbs, modifiers in noun phrases, adverbs, pronouns, interjections, and particles. To avoid redundancy, discussion of modifiers in noun phrases is postponed to chapters 3 and 4.

2.1. Nouns

Nouns and noun phrases, which are described in greater detail in chapter 3, fill the roles of subject, object, benefactive, location, time, manner, instrument/accompaniment, and nominal in predicate nominal constructions. The noun can be simple such as *wi?i* 'house' or a nominalized verb such as *tura-ri* (strong-DVB) 'strength'. The table in (67) summarizes the division of classes of nouns in Desano.

(67) Animate   Human   I. inherently male (end in i)
                             or female (end in *o*)
                         II. inflected for gender and number

               Nonhuman   I. group, take singularizer -*bɨ̃*
                         II. take plural -*a*

     Inanimate   I. non-countable
                         II. inherently plural, take a singularizer
                        III. take plural -*ri*

Simple nouns are of two basic classes: animate and inanimate. They differ in the following two ways: (1) their pluralizing and singularizing suffixes differ, as in (68); and (2) when an inanimate noun is subject, the verb ending is invariable, as in (69), and when an animate noun is subject, there is agreement of number and gender with the verb, as in (70).

(68)   weko   weko-a   wiʔi   wi-ri
           parrot   parrot-p   house   house-p
           parrot   parrots   house   houses

(69)   deko   ãʔrã-a   wi-ri   ãʔrã-a
           water   be-NON3^PRES   house-p   be-NON3^PRES
           There is water.   There are houses.

(70)   ɨbɨ   ãʔrĩ-bĩ   ɨbã   ãʔrĩ-bã
           man   be-3ms   men   be-3p
           There is a man.   There are men.

     The animate and inanimate classes are further subdivided on the basis of how plurality and gender are indicated. Animate nouns are divided into human and nonhuman with each of these having two subclasses.
     Group I human nouns are inherently either feminine or masculine. The masculine nouns usually end in *ɨ* and the feminine in *o*, such as *ɨbɨ* 'man', *dōbẽo* 'woman', *yēkɨ* 'grandfather', *yēkõ* 'grandmother'.
     Group II human nouns consist of a root plus a suffix which indicates gender and number: *-gɨ* (ms), *-go* (fs), *-rã* (ANp). For example, *bāhī-* 'child' when inflected with *-gɨ* (ms) becomes *bāhīgɨ* 'small boy'; when inflected with *-go* (fs) it becomes *bāhīgo* 'small girl'; and when inflected with *-rã* (ANp) it becomes *bāhīrã* 'children'. Nominalized verbs which are animate also fall into this category, e.g., *bāsīgɨ* 'the one (ms) who knows'. Many group II nouns are defective or irregular. For example, *bā-* 'progeny' inflects with *-gɨ* to become *bāgɨ* 'male progeny', and with *-go* to become *bāgo* 'female progeny', but *bā-* changes to *po-* when the animate plural suffix *-rã* is used, producing *porã* 'progeny (plural)'.[9]
     Nonhuman animate nouns are generally considered to be masculine unless the word *dōbẽo* 'woman' is added. The words *abe* 'sun' and *bupu* 'thunder' are considered animate and are inherently masculine. The

---

    [9]*bārā* shows up in the language as 'progeny (plural)' in the word for husband and wife: *bārāpo* 'wife' and *bārāpɨ* 'husband' probably come from *bā-* 'progeny', *-rã* (ANp) and *po* (a contracted term for *pago* 'mother') or *pɨ* (a contracted term for *pagɨ* 'father'), giving the meaning of 'mother of children' and 'father of children'.

Parts of Speech

nonhuman animates can be divided into two groups according to how they pluralize.[10] Group I are collective animate nouns that are inherently plural and require the singularizing suffix -bɨ to refer to a single member. Examples are bõbẽ 'bees', bõbẽ-bɨ 'bee', bɨrẽa 'mosquitoes', bɨrẽa-bɨ 'mosquito'. Group II nouns take the plural marker -a when the referent is plural, such as wekɨ 'cow', wekɨ-a 'cows'.

Inanimate nouns can be subdivided into three classes according to how they do or do not pluralize. Group I are mass nouns such as ɨbɨpa 'sand' and deko 'water' which are not countable. Group II nouns are inherently plural and take a singularizing suffix to refer to a single member. There are many irregularities in this category, but generally the singularizing suffix is the same as the classifier for that category. Examples are: weha 'paddles', weha-bu 'paddle'; gasi 'canoes', gasi-ru 'canoe'. The Desanos also often use -ri to pluralize members of this class, for example wehe-ri 'paddles'. Group III nouns take the regular plural -ri such as dia 'river', dia-ri 'rivers'; ɨtãye 'stone', ɨtãye-ri 'stones'.

Inanimate nouns can also be subdivided into classes according to their inherent characteristics, in particular their shape. Each of these classes is represented by its own classificatory marker. See §3.2 for a detailed discussion of noun classifiers.

2.2. Verbs

There are seven categories of verbs in Desano: copular, possessive, subjectless, intransitive, transitive, bitransitive, and verbs which take verbal complements including direct quotes (see §10.3).

The copular verbs are árĩ- 'be' and bārĩ 'not be'. They also function in predicate nominals, predicate adjectives, existential, locational, and possessive clauses. See §§7.2–7.4 for a discussion of these clauses.

The possessive verbs are opa- 'have' and bõo- 'not have'. Possessive verbs are discussed in §7.4.

There are no special verbs in Desano that always occur without a subject. There are, however, subjectless verb constructions which never express an overt subject, in which case the verb always carries the neuter (NON3) ending. Some verb constructions describing the weather are of this class.[11]

---

[10] Kaye (1970:91–92) argues that [+masc] and [+sing] are the unmarked members of the nominal gender/number system in Desano.

[11] Other constructions describing the weather do have a subject, however, such as: -bɨ (3ms) in bupu paa-gɨ ii-bɨ 'it is thundering' and -a (NON3ˆPRES) in deko bẽrẽ-ro ii-a 'it is raining'.

(71) asi-a
      be^warm-NON3^PRES
      It is warm.

The verb õã- 'good' is a subjectless verb in (72)–(73).

(72) õã-roka
      be^good-PROB^NON3
      It's okay.

(73) õʔã-a
      be^good-NON3^PRES
      It is good (used for thank you).

The verb wa-/waʔa 'go' occurs at times as a subjectless verb, in which case it does not function as a motion verb.

(74) eropa waʔa-bɨ
      thus go-NON3^PST
      That is how it went.

The verbs in (71)–(74) can also occur with an overt subject as in (75).

(75) ĩgɨ õʔã-bĩ
      he be^good-3p
      He is well.

Examples of intransitive or univalent verbs with only a subject argument include bodily function verbs and stative verbs expressing color and temporary states as illustrated in (76)–(82).

(76) bãhĩ-go   saʔri-bõ
      child-fs cough-3fs
      The child coughs.

(77) iri-ru   dia-bɨ
      this-CL   be^red-NON3^PST
      This (fruit) is red (went red).

(78) igo būkūbiri-bõ
 3fs be^happy-3fs
 She is happy.

(79) ĩgɨ gua-bī
 3ms be^angry-3ms
 He is angry.

(80) ẽrã ohokari-bã
 3p be^alive-3p
 They are alive.

(81) ohodɨka puʔri-a
 corn grow-NON3^PRES
 The corn grows/sprouts.

(82) yɨ bãgo bãsãdeyoa-bõ
 1s daughter be^born-3fs
 My daughter was born.

Other univalent verbs are stative verbs derived by the addition of -ya to transitive roots, see §6.2; verbs which involve patient subjects like 'fall, sink' as in (83); and the verb diasa 'be difficult' which occurs only with a nominalized sentential subject and thus only with neuter subject agreement as in (84)–(85).

(83) iri yukɨ yuʔri-diha-bɨ
 this tree fall-go^down-NON3^PST
 This tree fell to the ground.

(84) yɨʔɨ buʔe-ri diasa-bɨ
 1s study-DVB be^difficult-NON3^PST
 My studies are difficult.

(85) wiʔi bõʔbẽ-ri diasa-a
 house work-DVB be^difficult-NON3^PRES
 Building a house is difficult.

Furthermore, Desano has a variety of intransitive verb roots that indicate types of movement, whether it is uphill or downhill for example. These directional verbs of motion are listed in (86).

(86) bāhā-   'up a slight incline, including to the village from the river, no matter how steep the incline'
     bɨrī-   'up a steep incline'
     diha-   'down a steep incline'
     buʔa-   'down a slight incline'
     yuri-   'travel downriver'
     yāhā-   'enter inside'
     eha-   'arrive away from speaker'
     era-   'arrive towards the speaker'
     bāhī-   'turn and go in the opposite direction'
     taribuha- 'cross to the other side of a river or lake'

Transitive or bivalent verbs include such verbs as wēhẽ- 'kill', pa- 'hit', kūrī- 'bite', ābū- 'fix', and dore- 'order'.[12]

(87) Mandu-re   yɨ   tūgɨ   paa-di-gɨ   árī-bī
     Mandu-SPC 1s   brother   hit-PST-ms be-3ms
     My older brother hit Mandu.

(88) gɨa-re   dẽ   yuhu-gɨ   dore-biri-bī
     1x-SPC   first   one-ms   order-NEG-3ms
     No one ordered us even once.

The number of bitransitive or trivalent verbs in Desano is limited. The verbs -ārī 'say', were- 'tell', o- 'give', dua- 'sell', oʔo- or obeo- 'send', and buʔe 'teach' may take two objects, as in examples (89) and (90). In (89), the direct object is a verbal complement.

(89) ẽrã   õã-dore-beo-ra-re   gɨa-re   were-bī
     3p   beˆgood-order-send-DVB-SPC   1x-SPC   say-3ms
     He told us the greetings that they had sent.

(90) bārī   porā-re   Gõābɨ   ya-re   were-ro   gãʔbẽ-a
     1i   children-SPC   God   GEN-SPC   say-n   want-NON3ˆPRES
     We should tell our children God's Word.

A bivalent verb can be advanced to a trivalent verb with the addition of an oblique marked with -re (see §7.1), as in (91).

---

[12] Kaye (1970:73) states that no Desano verb roots have been found that are inherently both transitive and intransitive. In fact, there are a very limited number of verb roots that are both intransitive and transitive; yɨsɨ- 'be cold, make cold' and boho- 'be dry, dry' are among the few.

Parts of Speech

(91) gɨa-re gɨa colegio gɨa árī-ri-re biʔa-bã
 1x-SPC 1x school 1x be-DVB-SPC close-3p
 They closed up our being at school (didn't allow us to be at school anymore).

Verbs which take direct quote complements are the verbs *-árī* 'say' and *were-* 'tell', mentioned above as being bitransitive verbs, but they may also take direct quotes as discussed in §10.3.

2.3. Adverbs

Most adverbs are formed from the addition of *-ro* (deverbalizer) to verbal and other roots (§10.1). However, there are some other adverbial words as well as idiomatic adverbial expressions such as *doʔpa* 'yet/still', *dipaturi* 'again', *doʔpagã* 'today', *bāta* 'right away', *ipɨtɨ* 'very much', *bɨrigã* 'very much',[13] *diaye* 'right', and *kopɨ* 'left'.

The particle *dẽ* usually occurs sentence initial with the meaning of 'for the first time'. It frequently is combined with *goʔra* 'exactly', plus *-ge* (LOC) and/or *-re* (specifier) to give *dẽgoʔragere* 'at the beginning/a long time ago' or *dẽgere* with the same meaning.

(92) dẽ-goʔra-re ari-bɨ yɨʔɨ õ-ge-re
 first-exactly-SPC come-NON3^PST 1s here-LOC-SPC
 At the beginning I came here.

(93) dẽ iri-re ba-go ii-a
 first this-SPC eat-fs do-NON3^PRES
 This is the first time I am eating this.

The particle *dẽ* also occurs with negative verbs. The negative verb gives it the negative connotation of 'not once' or 'never'.

(94) Tomasu yɨ-re dẽ ii-tabū-biri-bī
 Thomas 1s-SPC first do-help-NEG-3ms
 Thomas didn't once help me! (he didn't begin helping me.)

The word *pɨɨ* occurs preceding a location or time word marked with the locative. It seems to indicate that the action of the verb takes place over a long stretch of travel or time.

---

[13] *bɨrigã* is derived from the verb root *bɨri-* 'be hard' plus *-gã* 'diminutive'.

(95) bāhã-bɨ   daha pɨɨ   dūpī-ya-ge
     goˆupriver-NON3ˆPST again long Nupi-river-LOC
     We went upriver again as far as the Nupi river.

(96) pɨɨ   gahi-dɨ̄-ge
     long   other-day-LOC
     until another day

The idiomatic expression in Desano *yuhudiayeta* composed of *yuhu* 'one' *diaye* 'right' and *ta* (limiter) could be termed an adverb. Its meaning seems to be 'without doing anything else'. Examples (97)–(98) illustrate its exact meaning.

(97) yuhu-diaye-ta   ba?a-bã   iri-poro-ri-re
     one-right-LIM   eat-3p   this-CL-p-SPC
     You just eat this (fruit) as it is without cooking it.

(98) yuhu-diaye-ta   seo-kā-ro   gã?bē-a
     one-right-LIM   plane-ABS-n   want-NON3ˆPRES
     (To make a large boat) you just plane it (without doing the other things that need to be done to prepare a small canoe).

In most of the occurrences of adverbs formed by the addition of *-ro* (inanimate deverbalizer), the construction is defined as an adverbial clause because it carries verbal arguments (see §10.4). There are some grammaticalized forms, however, that are defined as adverbial words rather than clauses such as those in (99)–(100).

(99) õã-ro
     beˆgood-DVB
     well

(100) tura-ro
      beˆstrong-DVB
      very much/greatly

When an adverb takes the suffixes *-ge* (locative) and *-re* (specifier) (§§4.2, 4.1), it describes a location or time. Without these suffixes, it describes the manner of an action. Examples (101)–(102) illustrate this.

(101) õã-ro   waʔa-bĩ
      be^good-DVB go-3ms
      He goes well.

(102) õã-ro-ge   waʔa-bĩ
      be^good-DVB-LOC   go-3ms
      He goes to a good place.

When the suffixes -ro-pa are added to the roots *yuhu-* 'one' and *gahi-* 'other', two common manner adverbs are formed as in (103) and (105). In (104) -ro occurs without -pa to give a different meaning.

(103) yuhu-ro-pa   ii-bã
      one-DVB-MAN   do-3p
      They do in the same way.

(104) yuhu-ro   ii-bã
      one-DVB   do-3p
      They do it together/in the same place.

(105) gahi-ro-pa   ii-bã
      other-DVB-MAN   do-3p
      They do otherwise/differently (has a negative connotation).

Adverbs formed with -ro-pa can also occur as the complement in a predicate nominal, as in (106), where it still seems to have an adverbial function.

(106) gahi-ro-pa   ãʔrã-a
      other-DVB-MAN   be-NON3^PRES
      It is otherwise.

When -pa is added to the locative demonstrative pronouns *e-ro* 'there' and *õʔõ* 'here' (§2.4), two manner adverbs are formed that are deictic and perform an anaphoric and cataphoric function respectively in the discourse.

(107) ero-pa   ii-bã
      there-MAN   do-3p
      They do like that.

(108) ō-pa   ii-bã
　　　here-MAN do-3p
　　　They do like this.

2.4. Pronouns

Desano pronouns are subdivided into personal, reflexive, demonstrative, and interrogative pronouns. The pronouns agree in gender, number, and animacy with their referents.

The personal pronouns indicate person, number, and, in the third person, gender. In the case of the first person plural, inclusive and exclusive are also distinguished. These are listed in (109). They may occur as head in a noun phrase (110) or as modifier of a head noun (111).

(109) Personal pronouns

	singular	plural
first person	yɨʔɨ	gɨa (exclusive)
		bārī (inclusive)
second person	bɨ̃ʔɨ	bɨ̃ã
third person	ĩgɨ (m)	ĩrã/ẽrã
	igo (f)	

(110) ĩgɨ   waʔa-bĩ
　　　3ms go-3ms
　　　He went.

(111) ĩgɨ   Manuel waʔa-bĩ
　　　3ms Manuel go-3ms
　　　This Manuel went.

Reflexive pronouns are formed by adding *basi* 'self' to the personal pronouns, e.g., *ĩgɨ basi* 'he himself'.

Demonstrative pronouns distinguish between animate and inanimate, and two degrees of distance. They are inflected for number and gender or class. In addition, there are two anaphoric demonstrative pronouns. The table in (112) lists the demonstrative pronouns.

Parts of Speech

(112) Demonstrative pronouns

	animate			inanimate	
	m	f	p	thing	location
proximate 'this one'	ĩʔĩ	igo	õã	i	õʔõ
distant 'that one(s)'	sĩʔĩ	sigo	sõã	si	sõʔõ
'the other'	gahi-gɨ	gahi-go	gahi-rã	gahi-[14]	

The animate demonstrative pronouns most frequently occur alone. The inanimate pronouns occur alone if they are referring to a concept or a general item; otherwise they occur with a classifier.

(113) sĩʔĩ   ãʔrĩ-bĩ
that^ms be-3ms
That's him there.

(114) gahi were-dia-k-a   bɨã-re
other say-DESID-ASSUM-NON3^PRES 2p-SPC
I want to tell you something else.

(115) gahi-yẽ ãsũ-bɨ
other-CL   buy-NON3^PST
I bought another/different one (dress).

(116) gasiru si-ru   õã-ri-ru   ãʔrã-a
canoe   that-CL be^good-DVB-CL be-NON3^PRES
That canoe is a good canoe.

(117) i-re   bɨã-re   were-a
this-SPC 2p-SPC say-NON3^PRES
I tell you this.

The anaphoric demonstrative pronouns are *iri* 'this' and *i-ro/e-ro* 'there'. The variation *i-ro/e-ro* reflects dialectical differences. *iri* has the meaning of 'this or that which was already referred to' and generally occurs with classifiers as in (118). *i-ro/e-ro* has the meaning of 'there or that place' and almost always is followed by *-ge* and /or *-re* as in (119).

---

[14] Although 'other' is generally considered a classifier, Malone considers 'other' to be a demonstrative pronoun in Tuyuca (personal communication).

(118) *wa-bɨ*   Jaime ya   *wiʔi-ge*   *iri-wiʔi-ge*   *eha*
go-NON3^PST Jim   GEN house-LOC this-house-LOC arrive
We went to Jim's house. Arriving at this/that house...

(119) *ero-ge-re*   *gɨa*   *árɨ-bɨ*
there-LOC-SPC 1x be-NON3^PST
We were there, at that place.

The interrogative pronouns distinguish animacy, number, and gender or class. Many of them are formed by prefixing *d-* to the demonstrative pronouns. They are presented in (120) and discussed further in chapter 8.

(120) Interrogative pronouns

animate

	masculine	feminine	plural
who	*dīʔī*	*digo*	*dōã*[†]
which one(s)	*yēʔebɨ*	*yēʔebõ*	*yēʔebārā*
how many			*dōã dɨkɨ*

[†]*doã* is also used if the 'who' is indefinite.

inanimate

what	*yēʔē*
where	*dōʔõ*
which one(s)	*di* + classifier
how much, many	*dipē*
how, what	*doʔpa*
why	*doʔpii/duʔpii* (*doʔpa* + *ii-* 'do')

2.5. Interjections

Desano closely resembles Barasano (Jones and Jones 1991:39) in its use of interjections. As in Barasano, they can be classified according to their mood: imperative, indicative, exclamatory, and dubitative.

The imperative interjection *idã* 'let's go', is used when the speaker expects the hearer to leave along with him. It can also be a leave-taking used when the speaker expects the addressee(s) to go a little later to the same destination.

(121) idã   bãhã-rã
      let's^go go^up-ANp
      Let's go up!

There are three indicative interjections in Desano. ã?ã indicates a positive response to a question as in (122); hai̧ indicates a positive response to a command or to a proposed plan as in (123); and bã 'That's it!' is used when a task is finished as in (124).

(122) ba-gi̧   ii-ri   ã?ã
      eat-ms do-Q   yes
      Are you eating? Yes!

(123) bi̧-sã   wa-ke   hai̧
      2s-also go-IMP   OK
      You go also. OK!

(124) bã   tu?a-ha-bi̧   bãrĩ
      that's^it finish-TEL-NON3^PST   1i
      That's it! We've finished.

There are many exclamatory interjections which seem to be used more by the women than the men. Some of the more commonly used interjections are listed in (125).

(125) a?ga   (expressing pain)
      a?yu   (expressing surprise, fear)
      abi̧   (expressing surprise)
      ade   (expressing surprise over something small, or a small amount)
      akerã (expressing surprise over a large amount, e.g., a lot of fish)
      kurã   (expressing sympathy)
      kue   (expressing being overwhelmed, not being sure one can handle it)

The dubitative interjection ūba 'doubt' may occur alone or be followed by the sentence 'I/we don't know' or with a sentence using the assumed evidential.

(126) dõʔõ-ge waʔa-ri   ũba   bãsĩ-biri-k-a
      where-LOC go-Q   doubt know-NEG-ASSUM-NON3^PRES
      Where did (he) go?   I don't know!

2.6. Particles

Particles that indicate contrast, addition, limiting, etc., are discussed in chapter 11.

3

Noun Phrase and Noun Phrase Operations

This chapter discusses the following constituents of the noun phrase: nouns, classifiers, the article *dipa-*, quantifiers, numerals, diminutives, augmentatives, genitive constructions, descriptive modifiers, plurals, postpositions, and limiters. Pronouns are discussed in §2.4. The case markers on the noun phrase differ from postpositionals in that they cannot stand alone and they are attached to the postpositionals when they both occur in the NP. These are discussed in chapter 4.

3.1. Nouns

Nouns are simple nouns, as discussed in §2.1, or forms derived from verbs by the addition of the deverbalizers *-ri* and *-ro* to form inanimate nouns, and the nominalizing suffixes *-gɨ* (masculine singular), *-go* (feminine singular), and *-rã* (animate plural) to form animate nouns. The resulting nouns, especially concrete nouns like *wɨ-ri-ru* (fly-DVB-CL) 'airplane', are a minimal manifestation of deverbalized clauses which are discussed in §10.1.

3.2. Noun classifiers

The modifiers within the noun phrase in Desano agree with the head noun. This is accomplished by an elaborate system of noun classifiers. Shape and physical categories distinguish the largest inanimate noun classes. The three animate classifiers denote masculine singular, feminine singular, and plural. Both inanimate and animate classifiers occur as suffixes on numerals, quantifiers, demonstrative pronouns, nouns, genitives, and verbs. With verbs, the inanimate classifier is suffixed to a verb root or stem following the deverbalizer as in (127); the animate classifier is suffixed directly to the verb root or stem as in example (128).

(127) pūgɨ　　　yɨʔɨ　āsū-ri-**gɨ**　opa-a
　　　hammock　1s　buy-DVB-CL　have-NON3ˆPRES
　　　I have the hammock that I bought.

(128) õã　　bãsã　　wai-re　　āsū-**rã**　　ãʔrĩ-bã
　　　these　people　fish-SPC　buy-ANp　be-3p
　　　These people are ones who buy fish.

A noun attached to the classifier defines the classifier as in examples (129), (131), and (133).

(129) yukɨ-**sārīrõ**
　　　trees-fence
　　　wood fence

Classifiers function in two ways: (1) to form a descriptive phrase about the referent noun as in (130), and (2) to form a referent noun that heads the noun phrase as in (131). The descriptive word formed with the classifier can replace the head noun if the speaker assumes that the hearer knows the referent.

(130) igo　ya　　suʔri-ro　　õã-rī-**yẽ**　　ãʔrã-a
　　　3fs　GEN　clothes-s　beˆgood-DVB-CL　be-NON3ˆPRES
　　　Her dress is pretty (lit., is a pretty (dress)).

(131) kōbē-**soro**　　　wehe-ri-**da**
　　　iron-CL　　　　fish-DVB-CL
　　　aluminum pot　fishline

Classifiers in Desano form a single phonological word with the root or stem to which they are suffixed. Nouns in Desano that do not have a representative classifier function as classifiers in that they attach to the same roots and stems as a classifier to form a single phonological descriptive word. The attached noun usually is slightly different from its representative noun in length or stress. These nouns are not included in the listing of classifiers unless they have extended definitions. Note the example of the noun *gobe* 'hole' in (132) that functions as its own classifier but also has an extended definition as shown in (133).

(132) *iri-gobe   ĩʔkã-ri-gobe   ã?rã-a*
this-hole deep-DVB-hole be-NON3^PRES
This is a deep hole.

(133) *disiporo-gobe*
door-hole
doorway

A listing of the nine categories of Desano inanimate classifiers is given in (134) with the number of classifiers for each category given in parentheses.

(134) shape (41)   geographical (14)
      masses/arrangements (18) abstract (3)
      designs (12)   associative (10)
      botanical (6)   general (3)
      disassociated parts (2)

Shape. The forty-one shape classifiers are subdivided into fourteen major groups as listed in (135)–(148).

(135) concave bowl, pot shapes

-soro	'bowl, pot'	bãta-soro	'clay bowl'
-koaru	'gourd'	yuhu-koaru	'one gourd'
-koro	'shell, basket'	wɨhɨ-koro	'woven reed basket'
-pa	'plate, chalice'	iʔri-ri-pa (drink-DVB-CL)	'chalice'

(136) protrusion/mound-shaped/hump

-buru	'hill'	ĩbã-ri-buru (be^high-DUB-hill)	'high hill'
-bu/bũ	'elliptic'	weha-bu	'paddle'
		uti-bu	'hornet nest'
		ĩtã-bũ	'rapids'

(137) crooked shapes

-kawe	'bent'	yukɨ-kawe	'crooked tree'
-subi	'bumpy/curly'	wãkĩ-ri-subiri	'hives'
		poari-subiri	'curly hair'
-sawe	'half-moon'	gãbĩro-sawe	'outer rim of ear'
-tĩʔkõ	'dented'	dataru yuhu-tĩʔkõ	'dented tin can'

(138) types of circles

-bero	'empty circle'	sã-ri-bero (put^on-DVB-CL)	'ring'
-se	'small filled-in circle'	biʔa-ri-se (close-DVB-CL)	'button'
-ti	'larger filled-in circle'	biʔa-ri-ti	'lid'

(139) spherical/tubular/cylindrical shapes

-ru	'spherical or oblong'	gasi-ru (bark-CL)	'canoe'
-diu	'egg'	õãri-diu	'good egg'
-tũrũ	'rolled-up cylinder'	goha-ra-tũrũ (write-DVB-CL)	'scroll'
-bora	'post'	wiʔi-bora	'pillar'
-turu	'log, barrel'	yukɨgɨ-turu (tree-CL)	'tree trunk (after being cut and trimmed)'
-poro	'cylinder with curved ending'	oho-poro	'banana'
		ĩgũrõ-poro	'toucan beak'
-tore	'hollow cylinder'	yukɨgɨ-tore	'hollow log'
		toa-tore	'drum'

(140) boxes or rectangular-shaped package

-pore	'package, bundle'	ĩbĩsĩri-pore	'package of candies'
		dĩhĩ-pore	'pregnant stomach'
		bũhĩ-pore	'bundle of leaves'
-pẽro	'box'	palitu-pẽro	'box of matches'
		doa-ri-pẽro (sit-DVB-CL)	'bench'
-kõbõrõ	'box'	oho-kobõrõ	'suitcase'

Noun Phrase and Noun Phrase Operations

(141) flat planes

-bīhī	'thin plane, sometimes pointed'	yōsē-ri-bīhī (spear-DVB-CL)	'spear'
-pãbē	'flat, connected'	bōhōtō-pãbē	'palm of hand'
		bi?ari-pãbē	'closed door'
-kaya	'platform'	papera du?peo-ri-kaya (paper place-DVB-CL)	'shelf'
-yẽ	'flat, thin, flexible'	su?ri õã-rī-yẽ	'nice clothes'
-gasiro	'sheet, skin, bark'	go-gasiro	'sheet of plastic'
-pũ	'leaf'	papera-pũ	'sheet of paper'

(142) pointed shapes

-waka	'dart'	baha waka-ri	'many darts'

(143) funnel shapes

-kusaro	'horn'	yābā wia-ri-kusaro	'large horn of deer'
-pero	'funnel'	weko-pero	'beak of parrot'
-doro	'funnel'	pũ-pero/pũ-doro	'paper made into funnel shape'

(144) thin long shapes

-poa	'hair'	yoa-ri-poa	'long hair'
-bã	'path'	ĩgĩ wa-ri-bã	'his going trail'
-da	'string'	sĩgã-da	'vine'
-si	'a piece of something round and long'	wai-si	'piece of fish'
		ta?be-tara-si	'cut off branch'

(145) hour glass shapes

-yu?iro	'tarantula, basket in hour-glass shape'	wia-ri-yu?iro	'large basket'

(146) diagonal

-si	'diagonal'	yukigi-si	'leaning tree'

(147) y-shaped

    -sẽrẽ   'y-shaped'   bã-sẽrẽ   'trail that branches off in two directions'

(148) crest

    -wɨaro   'crest of bird or comb'   ya?a-wɨaro   'my comb'

Masses or arrangements. Classifiers of mass refer to groups, bunches, swarms, flocks, piles, and rows as listed in (149).

(149)

-kuru	'group'	yese-kuru	'herd of pigs'
-turi	'stack'	papera-turi	'book'
-tõ	'cluster'	oho-tõ	'hand of bananas'
		bõhõ-tõ	'hand'
-ba	'pair'	pira yuhu-ba	'one pair of batteries'
-ka	'things arranged in a row'	tiari-ka	'wall'
-doto	'tied up bundle of sticks'	pea-doto	'bundle of firewood'
-boga	'bundle of vine-like things'	o?a-ri-boga (sweep-DVB-CL)	broom
-bu	'pile'	ĩtã-bu	'pile of rocks' (same as basket shape)
-tibi	'thin items curled up'	bõhõ-tibi	'fist'
-yɨbɨ	'clump'	ebo-yɨbɨ	'lump of clay'
		sĩ?ĩ-yɨbɨ (that^ms-CL)	'that fat man'
-yiri	'not quite closed'	disiro-yiri	'mouth partially opened'
-yɨsɨ	'ball or bundle of something soft'	gãrɨ-yɨsɨ	'ground-up cane'
-butu	'string, vine wound into a bundle'	sĩgã-butu	'bundle of vine'
-sãrĩrõ	'fence'	yukɨ-sãrĩrõ	'wood fence'
-guiri	'large substance'	ẽhõ-guiri	'large amount of phlegm'
		sĩgã yoari-guiri	'very long vine'
-butu	'crumpled mass'	su?ri-butu	'wrinkled up clothes'

-kẽ	'package'	būrū-kẽ	'tobacco leaves wrapped up'
-taribu	'separated-off area, room'	wɨa-ri-taribu	'large room'

Designs. The design classifiers are taken from descriptions of designs on animals and insects and are listed in (150). Some of these designs refer to the shape of objects as well as their design and are repeated in other lists. Such classifiers are marked with an asterisk.

(150) -tobe   'blotchy'
      -yɨrɨ   'stripe around'
      -doro*   'sharply defined, small design, usually round, funnel shape'
      -goho   'larger, irregular, indistinct design'
      -bã*   'strip along body, path (thin, long shape)'
      -subi*   'bumpy, also refers to curly (crooked shape)'
      -sawe*   'curved, ear-shaped (crooked shape)'
      -bero*   'circular'
      -bara   'small swirls'
      -taribu* 'elongated, separated areas of color (arrangements)'
      -sare   'fanned out, tail of the peacock or turkey'
      -dɨtɨ   'scaly', also means 'fish scales'

Botanical

(151)	-yũ	'palm'	oho-yũ	'banana plant'
	-gɨ (singular)	'tree'	pūgɨ̃	'hammock'
	-yukɨ (plural)	'trees' (also refers to hammocks, large sticks, and mountains)	pū-yukɨ	'hammocks'
	-kura	'rings on tree or palm'	ɨri-yũ-kura	'rings on palm tree'
	-goro	'flower'	diari-goro	'red flower'
	-sari	'stalk'	yuhu-sari	'one stalk'

Disassociated parts

(152)	-poga	'fine particles'	pea-poga	'sawdust'
	-bōhō	'fine crumbs or powder'	poga-bōhō	'crushed manioc flour'

Geographical

(153)	-bẽ	'place where there is or has been a fire'	pea-bẽ	'wood fire'
	-goro	'area where a house used to be or area used in some way'	wiʔi-goro	'location where house used to be'
	-pɨ	'place'	gahi-pɨ	'another place'
	-ya	'river, stream'	dĩbã-ya	'Poison River'
	-tɨro	'edge of'	dia-tɨro	'river bank'
	-waya	'canal'	eʔya-ri-waya	'wide canal'
	-sabe	'swampy area'	yoa-ri-sabe	'long swampy area'
	-dõʔkẽ	'bend in river, arc-like path in dance'	dia-dõʔkẽ	'bend in river'
	-yabu	'wide place in river, also handle on axe'	kõbẽ-yabu	'axe handle'
	-tɨrɨ	'precipice'	dia-tɨrɨ	'steep river bank'
	-kope	'back-water'	dia-kope	'back-water of a river'
	-yuri	'channel'	eʔya-ri-yuri	'wide channel'
	-põrẽ	'v-shaped projection'	tãrĩkẽ-põrẽ	'package of fish in v shape'
	-buru	'hill'	dipa-buru	'a hill'

Abstract (for time and place)

(154)	-dɨ̃	'day'	yuhu-dɨ̃	'one day'
	-subu	'time'	iri-subu	'this time' (see also §10.2)
	-bohe	'time' (has limited usage)	iri-bohe-ge (this-time-LOC)	'a long time ago'
			goe-ri-bohe (return-DVB-time)	'noon'

Associative

(155)	-ro/ru	'certain body appendages'	gãbĩ-rõ	'ear'
			guburo	'foot'
	-gasiro	'skin, bark' (repeated under shape)	yukɨ-gasiro	'tree bark'
	-dɨpɨ	'torso of animate bodies, limb of tree'	yaʔa-dɨpɨ	'my body'
	-kuru	'elbow, knee, tied knot'	diri-ri-kuru	'tied knot'

-yɨ̃gɨ	'calf of leg'	wekɨ-yɨ̃gɨ	'leg of cow'
-yuri	'crippled portion'	sĩʔĩ-yuri	'that crippled one'
-gõã	'bone'	dũʔrĩ-ri-gõã	'broken bone'
-diro	'meat'	dipa-diro	'piece of meat'
-wɨaro	'crest' (repeated under shape)	kãrẽyã-wɨaro	'comb of chicken'
-dɨka	'arm, fruit'	bõhõtõ-dɨka	'arm'

General. The three general classifiers are used to refer to nonspecific items and frequently are employed to form new expressions for foreign objects. They are: -yẽ 'thing' (also used for flat, thin shape) as in (156); -pẽ 'thing' formed from pa-yẽ, still used in some dialects and used in some special expressions such as in (157)–(158); and -dõhõ 'thing that has reference to being like another' illustrated in (159). (The boleka dialect deletes the -ho giving dõ-re.)

(156) kere   pee-ri-yẽ
      news   hear-DVB-CL
      radio

(157) di-pẽ/di-pa-yẽ
      which-CL
      How much?

(158) iri-pẽ/iri-pa-yẽ
      this-CL
      This is it/this is all.

(159) iri-dõhõ-re   opa-a
      this-thing-SPC   have-NON3^PRES
      I have this thing.

Example (160) illustrates the potential for various classifiers to be added to one noun.

(160) oho	'banana'	pea	'firewood'
oho-ru	'one banana'	pea-gɨ	'gun'
oho-yũ	'banana plant'	pea-ye	'ammunition'
oho-tõ	'hand of bananas'	pea-bẽ	'fire'
oho-pũ	'banana leaf'	pea-bãsã	'nonindigenous people'

Jones and Jones (1991:49–58) and Barnes (1990:273–92) have published extensive write-ups on the noun classifying system in Barasano and Tuyuca respectively, although, as in Desano, there is more that could be done. Barasano, Desano, and Tuyuca do not always have the same correlates between the classifier and its referent noun. For example, in Tuyuca the classifier for paddle is the same shape classifier as that of a machete, whereas, in Desano it is the same shape classifier as that of a deep basket. In Barasano, the classifier for paddle is the same classifier used in Desano for a flat, thin, flexible shape -yẽ.

3.3. The article *dipa-*

dipa- is a root that can occur with all classifiers to form a noun. Jones and Jones (1991:58) state for Barasano that it is "used...to refer to an object without naming the object itself." In Desano it gives an identity to the classifier and seems to have the meaning of the indefinite article 'a', as in (161)–(162).

(161) *dipa-tõ   igi-tõ   wɨa-ri-tõ   ãhrã-a*
     a-bunch grape-bunch large-DVB-bunch be-NON3^PRES
     A bunch of (tree grapes) is large.

(162) *dɨgɨ-ge   dipa-sabe   boca-bɨ   gɨa*
     jungle-LOC a-swampy^area find-NON3^PST 1x
     We found a swampy area in the jungle.

3.4. Quantifiers

There are three quantifiers in Desano: 'many', 'few', and 'all'.[15] The quantifier in Desano for individual items is *baha* 'a lot'; *baha* in its various forms occurs alone, or precedes or follows its noun referent with which it shows agreement, as in (163)–(165). To indicate 'very many' extra stress and length is put on the stressed syllable: *baháa*. When the referent is animate, *baha* takes the animate plural *-rã*, *baha-rã* 'many' as in (166).

(163) *kĩ   baha   buʔu-bã*
     manioc^root a^lot soak-3p
     They soak a lot of manioc roots.

---

[15]'Other' is not considered a quantifier in Desano. See §9.4 for quantifier negation. 'None' does not exist as a quantifier but, instead, is expressed indirectly by means of an inherently negative verb. See §9.2.

Noun Phrase and Noun Phrase Operations

(164) bāta-bīhī-ri baha-bīhī-ri
knife-CL-p a^lot-CL-p
many knives

(165) baha-re sora-bā
a^lot-SPC cook-3p
They cook a lot (of the palm-fruit).

(166) bāsā baha-rã
people a^lot-ANp
many people

To say 'a few', the negative marker -bẽ is added to *baha*, *baha-bẽ*, with the same rules as above. Quite frequently the diminutive marker -gā (§3.6) is added.

(167) baha-bẽ-gā-dɨ-ri
a^lot-NEG-DIM-day-p
a few days

(168) baha-bẽ-rã wa?a-bā
a^lot-NEG-ANp go-3p
A few (people) went.

To say 'a large amount' of a mass, the verb root *wɨa-* 'be^large' is used with the deverbalizer *-ro*, *wɨa-ro*.

(169) bõã wɨa-ro opa-a
salt be^large-DVB have-NON3^PRES
I have a large amount of salt.

To say 'a small amount' of a mass, *bẽro* 'a little' is used, often with the addition of the diminuitive *-gā*, *bẽro-gā*.

(170) bẽro-gā aī-bā
a^little-DIM take-3p
They take a little (referring to a mixture).

To say 'all' or 'everyone', the verb *árī-* 'to be' is followed by the totality aspect marker *pe?re-* 'be complete' (§5.5) plus the inanimate deverbalizer *-ri* as in (171) or the plural animate deverbalizer *-rã* as in (172).

(171) árĩ-pe?re-ri-re bu?e-bɨ
      be-TOTAL-DVB-SPC study-NON3ˆPST
      We studied everything.

(172) bira-rã   wa-bɨ   árĩ-pe?re-rã
      play-ANp go-NON3ˆPST be-TOTAL-ANp
      We all went to play (soccer).

3.5. Numerals

Numerals consist of a stem plus the inanimate classifier or animate gender and number marker that is appropriate for the head noun. They generally follow the head noun, but also can precede it, and may replace it.

Desano speakers use a quintenary system in which they count to five on one hand, then start at six by saying 'one hand plus one' up to ten. From there they count on their feet up to the number twenty. After that it is *baha* 'a lot'. Most Desanos now use the Spanish numbering system after the number 'four', and some speakers use the Spanish system for all numbers. The number stems are given in (173), using the inanimate classifier *-ya* 'river' and the animate endings for illustrative purposes. (With 'four', the deverbalizer *-ri* is also used before inanimate classifiers; the inanimate plural *-ri* is not used until the number 'four'.)

(173) Numerals

	number		animate ending/'river'
yuhu-		'one'	-gɨ (m)/-ya
			-go (f)/-ya
pe-		'two'	-rã (ANp)/-ya
i?re-		'three'	-rã/-ya
wapɨkɨ-		'four'	-rã/-ri-ya-ri
			(DVB-river-p)
yuhu bõhõtõ-kɨ-bãhã-		'five'	-rã/-ya-ri
(one hand-VB-PERT-)			
yuhu bõhõtõ-kɨ-bãhã gahi bõhõtõ yuhu-ru bãhã-		'six'	-rã/ya-ri
(one hand-VB-PERT other hand one-CL PERT-)			

pe bōhōtō-kɨ-bāhā gahi bōhōtō pe-ru bāhā-	'seven'	-rã/-ya-ri
pe bōhōtō-kɨ-bāhā gahi bōhōtō ɨre-ru bāhā-	'eight'	-rã/-ya-ri
pe bōhōtō-kɨ-bāhā gahi bōhōtō wapikɨ-ri-ru bāhā-	'nine'	-rã/-ya-ri
pe-pɨ-ri bōhōtō-kɨ bāhā- (two-place-p hand-VB PERT-)	'ten'	-rã/-ya-ri
guburi pe?re-ri bāhā- (feet finish-DVB PERT-)	'twenty'	-rã/-ya-ri

3.6. Diminutives and augmentatives

The diminutive -gã may be added to nouns (174)–(175), noun classifiers (176), or adverbs (177). To specify 'very little', accent and length fall on the syllable preceding the diminutive. In example (175) stress and length on -go would mean 'a very little one'.

(174) wai-gã   ba-ke
      fish-DIM   eat-IMP
      Eat the little fish!

(175) bĩ-go-gã   ã?rĩ-bõ
      little-fs-DIM   be-3fs
      She is a little one.

(176) goru   bĩ-ri-ru-gã
      ball   little-DVB-CL-DIM
      little ball

(177) bia   dabero-gã   ii-bã   iri   deko-re
      pepper   aˆlittle-DIM do-3p   this   water-SPC
      They put a little hot pepper in the soup.

The augmentative -ro may be added to nouns to indicate increased size. It is used less than the diminutive. When added to nouns the accent is drawn to the syllable preceding -ro as in (178).

(178) wɨa-gɨ-ro   ã?rĩ-bĩ
      large-ms-AUGMENTATIVE   be-3ms
      He is very large.

3.7. Genitive constructions

Desano has alienable and inalienable possession. Alienable possession uses the case marker *ya* (genitive) to express the kind of ownership which can be terminated. The phrase consists of possessor + *ya* + possessed or classifier referring to referent, as in (179)–(181). In (180), *ya?a* is a contraction of *yɨ?ɨ ya* (1s GEN).

(179) ĩgɨ   ya   wi?i
      3ms GEN house
      his house

(180) iri   kobõro   ya?a   (yɨ?ɨ ya)   kobõro   ã?rã-a
      this box   my   (1s GEN)   box   be-NON3^PRES
      This box is my box.

(181) igo   ya   dipuru   pũrĩ-yo-ro
      3fs GEN head   hurt-HSY-NON3
      Her head hurts.[16]

The genitive *ya* can occur alone without a head noun when referring to nonindividuated inanimate objects.

(182) igo   ya   ã?rã-a
      3fs GEN be-NON3^PRES
      They are her (hers)/things.

(183) ẽrã   ya-re   pee-a
      3p GEN-SPC hear-NON3^PRES
      I understand theirs (their language).

In referring to animate beings, particularly one's pet, *ya* is followed by gender-number markers.

(184) sĩ?ĩ   diaye   ĩgɨ   ya-gɨ   ã?rĩ-bĩ
      that^ms dog   3ms GEN-ms be-3ms
      That dog over there is his.

---

[16]To say 'her head hurts', it is more common for the genitive to be dropped and a specifier added to 'her': *dipuru pũrĩ-yo-ro igo-re* 'head hurts to her', thus "depriving an attached body part of categorical status by promoting the owner to one of the major grammatical elements of the clause" Hopper and Thompson (1984:725).

Noun Phrase and Noun Phrase Operations

ya is also used in connection with references to functions of humans, such as the captain of the village.

(185) *gɨa ya-gɨ capitan*
   1x GEN-ms chief
   our captain

For inalienable kinship relations, the possessor occurs directly before the possessed without *ya*. The possessive pronouns are the same as the other personal pronouns in Desano (§2.4).

(186) *yɨ yẽkõ*
   1s grandmother
   my grandmother

(187) *igo pago*
   3fs mother
   her mother

The Desanos often use the vocative forms of kinship terms when referring to a person, as well as in speaking directly to him or her. They do not indicate possession with the vocative forms. The possessed form for '(my) father' is *yɨ pagɨ*, and the vocative form is *aʔɨ*; the possessed form for '(my) older sister' is *yɨ tĩgo*, and the vocative is *diʔo*. Note the usage of these forms in (188)–(191).

(188) *yɨ pagɨ   yɨ bẽrã gua-bĩ*
   1s father 1s with be^angry-3ms
   My father was angry with me.

(189) *aʔɨ-sã   bãrĩ-bã*
   dad-also not^be-3p
   Dad (and the others) weren't there.

(190) *yɨ tĩgõ   gahi-bãkã-ge   árĩ-ku-bõ*
   1s older^sister other-town-LOC be-ASSUM-3fs
   My sister is at another town.

(191) *aʔri-ri   diʔo*
   come-Q sister
   Do you come, sister?

With nominalized verbs, the option generally does not exist to express the subject as possessor of the nominalized forms, as shown in (192)–(193). Example (192) can also be stated without the -ya. When it is, it has more the meaning of working for her children's future. Example (193) stated without the -ya carries no change of meaning.

(192) igo bõʔbē-bõ igo porã   ya   árī-bu-ri-re
     3fs work-3fs 3fs children GEN be-POT-DVB-SPC
     She works on behalf of her children, for her children's well-being.

(193) bɨʔɨ Gõābɨ ya   weredīgī-ri-re were-bɨ   gɨa-re
     2s God GEN talk-DVB-SPC say-NON3^PST 1x-SPC
     You told God's Word (God's speaking) to us.

The word *bāhā* 'pertaining to' could be considered a kind of genitive pro-noun. When it refers to inanimate objects, it occurs alone or with a classifier. When it refers to animate beings, it is marked for person and number.

(194) i   wiʔi   bāhā
     this house PERT
     things that belong to this house

(195) i   wiʔi   bāhā-gɨ
     this house PERT-ms
     the male person from this house

(196) õ   doka   bāhā-rã
     here below PERT-ANp
     the people from downriver

(197) buʔe-bɨ   karēyā   bāhā-re
     study-NON3^PST chicken PERT-SPC
     We studied things/information about chickens (their care, etc.).

(198) dɨkɨ-ri   bāhā-re   keo-bā
     heavy-DVB PERT-SPC weigh-3p
     They weighed the things that were heavy.

(199) kabã bāhã-yẽ
bed   PERT-CL
a sheet or blanket (lit., 'that flat, thin, flexible thing which pertains to a bed')

3.8. Descriptive modifiers

Like Barasano (Jones and Jones 1991:63), Desano is a verb-adjective language, meaning that there is a single set of roots which function either as verbs or adjectives. As verbs they take regular verbal inflection and serve as predicates, although they do not show the full range of tense/aspect/modal oppositions typically associated with verbs (Hopper and Thompson 1984:727), for example, (200). The verbal adjectives can take deverbalizers (see §10.1) and/or classifiers, and function within noun phrases. These modifiers usually follow the head noun as in (201). However, they most often replace the head as a relative clause or a nominalized form followed by a classifier as in (202)–(203).

(200) õʔã-bĩ
be^good-3ms
He is good/well.

(201) bia   dia-ri
pepper be^red-DVB
red pepper

(202) ĩgɨ̃   õã-gɨ   ãʔrĩ-bĩ
3ms be^good-ms be-3ms
He is a good person (lit., one who is good).

(203) õã-ri-dɨ   ãʔrã-a
be^good-DVB-day be-NON3^PRES
It is a good day.

There exists in Desano a small closed class of adjectival roots that never occur with verb endings but do occur with classifiers. These adjectives are age and dimension types and fit Dixon's generalization that age, dimension, value, and color types are likely to belong to the adjective class, however small it is (1982:46), although in Desano value and color are verbal roots. This class of adjectival roots includes bãbã- 'new', bĩ- 'small', bɨtã- 'small (used for plural items)', bɨrã- 'old', paga- 'large (used for plural items; for singular wɨa- takes verbal inflection). Other modifiers which occur with classifiers but never with verb endings are the demonstrative *gahi-* 'other' (§2.4), the quantifier *baha* 'a lot' (§3.4), and the pro-noun *bāhā* 'pertaining to' (§3.7).

3.9. Plurals

For both animate and inanimate nouns there is a regular way to pluralize, in addition to many irregular forms.

The majority of inanimate nouns are pluralized by the addition of the suffix *-ri*. This suffix occurs on both the head noun and any modifiers that accompany it; see also §2.1.

(204)   dĩ   diu-ri-pɨ   yẽ-ri-diu-ri   ã?rĩ-ri
        which   egg-p-FOC   be^bad-DVB-egg-p   be-Q
        Which eggs were the bad eggs?

Some examples of irregular ways of pluralizing are (1) for nouns that are spherical in shape and that take the classifier *-ru*, *dipa* is inserted between the noun and the classifier to form the plural, as in (205); (2) for nouns that end with the classifier *-gɨ* 'tree' the plural is formed by the addition to the root of *yukɨ* 'trees' as in (206)–(207); and (3) for some nouns whose singular ends in *-ru* or *-ro*, the *-ru* is changed to *-ri* to form the plural as in (208).

(205)   goru   godiparu
        ball   balls

(206)   gãrɨ-gɨ   gãrɨ-yukɨ
        sugar-cane   sugar-canes

(207)   pũ-gɨ   pũ-yukɨ
        hammock   hammocks

(208)   kuiru   kuiri   guburo   guburi
        eye   eyes   foot   feet

The majority of animate, nonhuman nouns form the plural with the suffix *-a*, as in (209).

(209)   wekɨ   wekɨ-a   tẽhẽ   tẽhẽ-a
        cow   cows   tick   ticks

Noun Phrase and Noun Phrase Operations

Other animate nouns are plural in themselves and have singularizing suffixes as described in §2.1, for example, (210). In (211) the word for 'man' is pluralized slightly differently; the two forms of the singular reflect dialectical differences.

(210) dōbẽ   dōbẽ-o
      women   woman

(211) ɨbɨ/ɨbɨgɨ   ɨbā
      man   men

The plurals for kinship terms are irregular in that for male relatives the plural is sɨbārā as in (212), and for female relatives the plural is sā dōbẽ 'also women' as in (213).

(212) ẽrā   pagɨ-sɨbārā
      3p   father-p
      their fathers (their ancestors)

(213) ẽrā   pago-sā   dōbẽ
      3p   mother-p women
      their mothers

The root used for 'sons' and 'daughters' is different from the root for 'son' and 'daughter' (see §2.1) This difference is reflected also in the plural for younger brothers and sisters as in (214)–(215).

(214) pagɨ   bāgɨ   pagɨ   porā
      father son   father   children
      brother   brothers or brothers and sisters

(215) pagɨ   bāgo   pagɨ   porā   dōbẽ
      father daughter   father   children   women
      sister   sisters

A proper name or kinship term plus the marker -sā 'also' (§11.2) gives a plural meaning 'in addition to the others' when the speaker knows that the hearer is aware of the people that would be with the person whose name is given, as in (216).

(216) a?ɨ-sã   bãrĩ-bã
      dad-also not^be-3p
      Dad (and the others) weren't there.

3.10. Postpositions

Postpositions are words that express spatial and temporal relations. These relators always occur after the noun and can carry the case marker *-re* (§4.1) and the locative *-ge* (§4.2). They are listed in (217) and illustrated in (218)–(220). The forms *kore* 'before' and *pi?rɨ* 'after' also occur in adverbial clauses (see §10.4) and *pi?rɨ* 'after' can occur sentence initially (§11.7).

(217) deko   'in the middle of'
       doka   'below'
       weka   'above'
       po?ro   'near'
       tɨro   'near' (edge of)
       kore   'before'
       po?eka   'inside'
       pi?rɨ   'after'
       ohogoro   'end point'
       watope   'in the midst of'

(218) Bogotá kore
      Bogotá before
      the other side of Bogotá

(219) dɨtaru deko
      lake   middle
      in the middle of the lake

(220) iri   pi?rɨ
      this after
      after this

The postpositional phrases may occur in a possessor relationship with *bãhã* 'pertaining to' (see §3.7).

(221) bũhĩ doka   bãhã-yẽ
      roof below PERT-CL
      the thing that belongs under the roof

(222) ero   kore   bāhã-rã
      there before   PERT-ANp
      the people from before/an earlier generation

The word *dopa* 'like' is a comparative postposition (§1.8). It follows both noun phrases and nominalized clauses and also occurs as part of manner adverbial clauses (see §10.5). In example (223) *dopa* follows a nominalized clause.

(223) ero   core   gɨa   árī-di-ro   dopa   árī-bea-a   pare
      there before 1x   be-PST-DVB   like   be-NEG-NON3^PRES   finally
      We are not like we were before.

3.11. Limiters

Limiters are words that occur following a noun and also following postpositional phrases. Their function is to limit the noun to a restricted set. They can carry the case markers *-re* and *-ge* for the whole noun phrase but do not occur with classifiers as other noun modifiers do. These limiters are *di?ta* 'only', *seyaro* 'just', as in 'just them', *go?ra* 'exactly', and *dɨkɨ* 'each'.

The forms *di?ta* and *seyaro* have somewhat the same meaning. The difference seems to be that when *di?ta* occurs with a noun there could be other items involved in the same action but, in fact, only this one/these ones are; *seyaro* seems to be indicating that the item is a closed group, i.e., there could not be any other items. Note the usage of these two limiters in (224)–(228).

(224) ẽrã   bẽrẽ   di?ta   ba?a-bã
      3p   fruit   only   eat-3p
      They eat only mere fruit.

(225) deko   bẽrã   di?ta   piu-bã
      water   with   only   pour-3p
      They pour in only water (to mix it).

(226) eropa   di?ta   gɨa-re   bãsɨ-kɨ   ii-bã
      thus   only   1x-SPC   know-SR   do-3p
      They caused us to know just (by doing) like that.

(227) gɨa bari seyaro
     1x food just
     just what we eat

(228) bɨhawere-yũ-bã   ẽrã seyaro duha-rã
     be^sad-ASSUM-3p 3p just   remain-ANp
     They were sad with just (the two of) them remaining behind.

The form *goʔra* is more a definer of the noun than a limiter, but grammatically it functions like a limiter as in (229). It is frequently used with numbers as in (230).

(229) ĩgɨ̃ kuiri tɨro   goʔra   paa-pɨ
     3ms eyes edge exactly hit-HSY^3ms
     He hit him right on the edge of his eye

(230) 43 goʔra   ãʔrã-bã
     43 exactly be-3p
     There were exactly 43 (students).

The form *dɨkɨ̃* 'each' is described as a limiter since it occurs after the noun and may take the case markers *-re* and *-ge*.

(231) bãsã   kuru-ri dɨkɨ̃ opa-bã ɨ̃rĩ-re
     people group-p each have-3p fruit-SPC
     Each people group has *ɨ̃rĩ* fruit.

4
Case

The case markers in Desano are the specific object marker *-re*, the locative marker *-ge*, and *bẽrã* 'with, accompaniment, instrument'. Both *-ge* and *bẽrã* may be followed by *-re*.

4.1. The specific object marker *-re*

The specific object marker *-re* occurs at the end of the noun phrase and marks specific, referential patients of transitive verbs, experiencers, and spatial-temporal expressions to establish a new frame and give further references to that frame. Examples (232)–(233) illustrate the occurrence of *-re* on specific, referential patients of transitive verbs. An example in which *-re* is not used because the patient is not specific is (235). Also *-re* is suffixed to object personal pronouns since these pronouns refer to specific individuals already on stage in the discourse (Malone 1982:34). For the same reason *-re* also occurs on the inanimate anaphoric pronoun *iri* 'this' as in (232).

(232) *iri-re   bãsĩ-dia-gɨ*
      this-SPC know-DESID-ms
      wanting to know this

(233) *bõã-re   ãsũ-bã*
      salt-SPC buy-3p
      They bought salt.

-re also occurs on relative clauses that function as patient, since their referent is specific as in (234).

(234) *poga* [*ẽrã bẽrõ o-beo-ra-re*] *aĩ*
manioc^cereal [3p small^amount give-send-DVB-SPC] carry

era-bĩ
arrive-3ms
He brought the small amount of manioc flour that they sent.

Examples (235)–(236) illustrate experiencers as recipients of bitransitive verbs, viz, indirect objects, since they too refer to specific individuals already on stage in the discourse.

(235) *yɨ-re bari o?o-bõ*
1s-SPC food give-3fs
She gives me food.

(236) *ĩgɨ bāgɨ-re sẽrẽpi-bĩ*
3ms son-SPC question-3ms
He asked his son.

Examples (237)–(239) illustrate *-re* occurring on experiencers when oblique constituents are advanced to status as indirect objects (see §6.1).

(237) *eropa wa-bɨ   gɨa-re*
thus go-NON3^PST 1x-SPC
It went thusly for us.

(238) *paru   pũrĩ-k-a   yɨ-re*
stomach hurt-ASSUM-NON3^PRES 1s-SPC
My stomach hurts. (lit., The stomach hurts to me.)

(239) *gɨa-re gɨa kolegio gɨa árĩ-ri-re bi?a-bã*
1x-SPC 1x school 1x be-DVB-SPC close-3p
They didn't allow us to be at school. (lit., They closed on us our being at school.)

The marker *-re* on spatio-temporal expressions in Desano establishes a specific frame in which a significant backbone event will occur. As the text moves along, the frame thus established may be replaced by another frame, also marked with *-re*. Many texts begin with a time word marked with *-re* and/or with a locative marked with *-re*. Example (240)

Case   59

shows the beginning line of a text which establishes the specific time and location for the backbone events which are about to be related.

(240) dē-re   ari-bɨ   yɨʔɨ   õ-ge-re
       first-SPC   come-NON3^PST 1s   here-LOC-SPC
       At the beginning I came here.

Later in the text, backbone events occur at another specific location, which consequently is also marked with -re.

(241) gɨa   yoa-ri-bohe   árī-bɨ   ero-ge-re   iri   bākā-ge-re
       1x   be^long-DVB-time   be-NON3^PST   there-LOC-SPC this   town-LOC-SPC
       We were a long time there in this town.

-re can occur on a reference to a specific location or time without the locative -ge being used (§4.2). In (242), the conference is the specific frame for the backbone event 'Jim arrived'.

(242) iri   conferencia-re   Jaime   eha-bī
       this conference-SPC   Jim   arrive-3ms
       Jim arrived at this conference.

For an example of a location not marked by -re because it is only being introduced to the discourse, see (244)–(245).

4.2. Locative marker

The locative marker -ge codes references to static locations as in (241), path in (243), goal in (245), and source in (244), particularly in connection with animate participants. It also is frequently attached to temporal expressions, when the reference is a point in time.

(243) yɨʔɨ wa-bɨ   yuhu-bā-ge
       1s   go-NON3^PST   one-trail-LOC
       I went on a trail.

(244) yukɨ-dɨpɨ-ge   gagidīgī   peya-bī
       tree-branch-LOC scream   be^perched-3m
       He (monkey) sat screaming on/from a tree branch.

With many constituents, the presence of -ge is obligatory to indicate that the constituent has locative reference. With expressions that are inherently spatio-temporal, however, its absence has the effect of defocusing the referent. In example (245), *-ge* does not occur on the first location 'here' because it was the second location 'a farm' that was the true goal (the place where 'we' were going to stay).[17]

(245) gɨa   ō-re   era   pɨʔrɨ   buʔa-bɨ   pare   finka-ge
      1x   here-SPC   arrive after   go^down-NON3^PST finally farm-LOC
      We arrived here, after which we went down to a farm (our final destination).

When *-ge* occurs with time words, a point along the spectrum of space and time rather than the source or goal is indicated. In example (246), the good day contrasts with the speaker saying that on a rainy day he won't be able to go, whereas example (247) is in the context of how and where they spent the earlier part of the day.

(246) ōā-ri-dɨ-ge   wa-gɨka
      be^good-DVB-day-LOC   go-PROB^1ms
      On a good day I will go.

(247) yābɨka-ge   buʔa-bɨ   finca-ge
      afternoon-LOC go^down-NON3^PST   farm-LOC
      In the late afternoon we went down to a farm.

Examples (248)–(250) come from a short text with two specific time frames, both of which are marked with *-ge* and *-re*. The first part of the text concerns what happened a long time ago when he was a child; the second describes what he does now since his father died. (In fact, *-ge* has become grammaticalized in the time words *doʔpage* 'now' and *iribohege* 'a long time ago'.) In example (250), *-ge* indicates a point in time.

(248) iri-bohe-ge-re   yɨʔɨ   bāhɨ-gɨ   árɨ-kɨ-ge-re
      this-time-LOC-SPC   1s   child-ms   be-SR-LOC-SPC
      A long time ago, when I was a child,...

---

[17] For a similar analysis in Barasano, see Jones and Jones (1991:71–72).

(249) *do?pa-ge-re yɨ pagɨ sīrī-ra pɨ?rɨ-ge yɨ-sã ẽrã ii-di-ro*
now-LOC-SPC 1s father die-DVB after-LOC 1s-also 3p do-PST-DVB

dopa-ta ii-a
like-LIM do-NON3^PRES
Now at this time since my father has died (being older), I also do like they used to do.

(250) *bābā bāsā-gɨ árī-gɨ-ge bõ?bẽ-kuri-bɨ*
new grow^up-ms be-ms-LOC work-travel-NON3^PST
At the point of time when I was newly grown up, I traveled working.

When *-ge* occurs in connection with a reference to an animate participant, it marks the source of the participant, as in examples (251)–(257).

(251) *ẽrã gɨa po?ro bāhā-rã-ge era-kɨ̃*
3p 1x near PERT-ANp-LOC arrive-SR
When people from near where we live arrived,...

(252) *ẽrã gɨa tɨ̃gɨ porã-ge árī-bã*
3p 1x brother children-LOC be-3p
They were the children from our older brother.

In example (253), the source of the spoken word was 'everyone'.

(253) *árī-bɨ árī-pe?re-rã-ge-ta gɨa*
say-NON3^PST be-TOTAL-ANp-LOC-LIM 1x
The source of what was said was everyone (all of us).

Example (254) seems to indicate the source of those not coming from other locations.

(254) *gahi-rã-ge ari-biri-bã*
other-ANp-LOC come-NEG-3p
People did not come from other places.

In (255), *-ge* occurs with both the subject and the location of the sentence. The source of the four men was 'different places', and they came together at their planned location.

(255) *iri   bā?ā   ohogoro-ge   gābē   bokatūri-bɨ   wapikɨ-rā-ge-ta*
      that trail end-LOC   RECIP meet-NON3ˆPST   four-ANp-LOC-LIM
      The four of us from different places met at the end of the trail.

In morphological causative constructions (§6.1), the causee of a transitive verb may appear as the source (an "oblique object" according to Comrie (1985:339)). Thus, in (256), 'our mothers' is the causee.

(256) *iri-re   gɨa   pago-sādōbē-ge-re   kōyōpo-dore*
      this-SPC   1x   mother-p-LOC-SPC   heat-order
      Ordering our mothers to heat this,...

In (257) the source is inanimate.

(257) *iri-ge-re   i?ri-biri-k-a*
      this-LOC-SPC   drink-NEG-ASSUM-NON3ˆPRES
      We don't drink from this (the juice from this fruit).

4.3. Instrument and accompaniment marker

The marker *bẽrã* 'with' indicates instrument and accompaniment or coparticipation. Examples are given in (258)–(259).

(258) *Bibiadō   Luciadō   bẽrã   wi?i-re   ii-bã*
      Vivian   Luciano   with   house-SPC   do-3p
      Vivian made the house along with Luciano.

(259) *deko   kóã-bã   balderi   bẽrã*
      water throwˆout-3p   pails   with
      They threw out the water with pails.

5
Verb Phrase

The Desano verb carries a great variety of nuances of meaning in a discourse because of its use of tense, evidentials, modals, aspectuals, locationals, some miscellaneous suffixes that add finer nuances, negation, verb-compounding, and several special phrases composed of a root plus an auxiliary specific to that phrase. Also, many of the noun phrases include or consist entirely of nominalized verbs that can carry many of the suffixes mentioned above.

The obligatory elements in the main verb are the verb stem, a tense-evidential suffix, and a suffix which carries subject agreement. In between these can occur almost any number of modal, aspectual, and other markers, including the negative (§9.1). The only restriction on the co-occurence of these markers is semantic. Examples (260)–(261) show some of the suffixes that occur between the verb stem and the evidentials.

(260) kãrĩ-dia-goʔra-biri-kã-yũ-bĩ
sleep-DESID-exactly-NEG-ABS-ASSUM-3m
It is assumed that he certainly didn't want to sleep.

(261) aĩ-a-dĩgĩ-dore-biri-bokũ-bĩ
carry-away-CONTIN-order-NEG-PROB-3ms
He may not continually order to carry it away.

The topics discussed in this chapter are agreement of subject and verb, tense evidentials, tense markers, imperatives, aspectuals, directionals, modal suffixes, miscellaneous suffixes, and auxiliary verbs. Verb compounding and denominalization are discussed at the end of this chapter.

5.1. Agreement

Agreement of person, number, gender, and animacy between subject and verb is required. It is shown by a set of suffixes of which the most common are -bõ (third-person feminine singular), -bĩ (third-person masculine singular), and -bã (third-person plural). There is a variety of suffixes which are the same for the other persons (first person, second person, and inanimate). Note on the table in (262) that the hearsay evidentials have different suffixes. These suffixes show agreement and are part of the evidential and tense marker system and occur in final position in the verb phrase. They are an anaphoric device in that they can constitute the only reference to an entity in the clause. More details on the suffixes are given in the next section.

5.2. Tense-evidentials

The evidential markers carry information about the tense, the subject, and how the speaker obtained his information. The evidentials used in Desano are listed in (262).

(262) Evidential markers

	visual	hearsay	assumed	inferred
past				
3fs	-bõ	-yu-po	-yũ-bõ	-di-go árĩ-bõ
3ms	-bĩ	-yu-pɨ	-yũ-bĩ	-di-gɨ árĩ-bĩ
3p	-bã	-yõ-rã	-yũ-bã	-di-rã árĩ-ma
other (NON3)	-bɨ	-yo-ro	-y-a	-di- árĩ-bɨ
present				
3fs	-bõ		-kõ-bõ	
3ms	-bĩ		-kũ-bĩ	
3p	-bã		-kũ-bã	
other	-a		-k-a	

In the nonthird person inferred evidential, the ending on the verb stem on the first part of the phrase agrees with the subject as to masculine (gɨ), feminine (go), plural (rã) and neuter/inanimate (ro). The inferred evidential is a verb phrase which consists of a subordinate verb nominalized by the suffix -di (past) plus a suffix that indicates gender, number, and animacy. This is followed by the verb árĩ- 'be', a distant or recent past marker, and the subject agreement marker.

Verb Phrase

There is fluctuation between -*yu*- and -*yo*- in the hearsay markers, and -*ku*- and -*ko*- in the assumed markers following the Desano system of vowel harmony (§1.16). Also, both -*ku*- and -*yu*- are nasalized from the suffixes on their right (§1.13). The *boreka porã* dialect of Desano does not pronounce the -*yu*- before -*po* and -*pɨ*. All the other dialects retain the -*yu*-. Kaye's (1970:101) statement that "the hierarchy formed by the reported (hearsay) endings resembles that of the participial endings rather than that of the personal endings" is borne out by the data here.

When interrogatives occur with the evidentials, the person marker is deleted and the question suffix -*ri* added (see §§8.1–8.2). The negative suffix can be used with each of the evidentials without a category shift occurring (see §9.1).

The four sets of evidentials (visual, hearsay, assumed, and inferred) are now discussed, together with the opinion suffix -*sõ*.

The visual evidential. The visual evidential lets the hearer know that the speaker himself experienced the event or was a witness to it. It is used also to express truths or states that the speaker can attest to from his experience. Some illustrations are given in (263)–(265).

(263) gɨa õ-ge-re   era-bɨ
      1x   here-LOC-SPC   arrive-NON3^PST
      We arrived here.

(264) Ñu   õã-gɨ   ã?rĩ-bĩ
      John be^good-ms   be-3ms
      John is a good person.

(265) deko   bẽrẽ-ro   ii-*a*
      water   fall-n   do-NON3^PRES
      It is raining.

The verb *kari*- with the visual evidential indicates that the speaker obtained his information from senses other than the visual. He feels without seeing, as in (266)–(267), and he hears without seeing, as in (268)–(269). The verb can occur alone but most often occurs with other verbs.

(266) bĩrĩ-a   wa-kari-a-bɨ
      drown-PERF   go-seem-PERF-NON3^PST
      (The boat overturned) and it seems I went under.

(267) yɨ-sã   õã-ro   ĩã-biri-kari-bɨ
      1s-also be^good-DVB see-NEG-seem-NON3^PST
      I also didn't see it very well (it was night).

(268) bupu   bɨsɨ-gɨ   kari-bĩ
      thunder noise-ms seem-3ms
      It is thundering (I can hear the thunder).

(269) poe   paa-gɨ kari-bĩ
      field hit-ms seem-3ms
      He is cutting down his field (I can hear an axe chopping).

The hearsay evidential. This evidential tells the hearer that the speaker obtained his information from someone else. There are no observed examples of the hearsay evidential occurring in first person, but occasionally it occurs with second person as in (273). Most commonly this evidential is used in connection with a past action. However, examples (271) and (272) show how this evidential sometimes occurs in connection with a present event.

(270) Bãdu   yɨ tĩgɨ-re   paa-pɨ
      Manuel 1s brother-SPC hit-HSY^3ms
      Manuel hit my older brother (hearsay).

(271) arroz 20 pesos waha-kɨ-yo-ro
      rice   20 pesos pay-VB-HSY-NON3
      Rice costs 20 pesos (I was told).

(272) Bãria wa?a-ri   wa-po
      Mary   go-Q   go-HSY^3fs
      Is Mary going?   She said she is going.

(273) bɨ?ɨ miercoles   árĩ-kɨ bõ?bẽ-a-yo-ro
      2s   Wednesday   be-SR   work-REC^PST-HSY-NON3
      You worked on Wednesday (I heard it from your wife).

The assumed evidential. The assumed evidential tells the hearer that the speaker has not seen or is not seeing the event, but supposes that an event has occurred or is occurring based on his knowledge of the habits of the persons involved, what they indicated they were going to do, or on his general knowledge of how things work. This evidential

Verb Phrase

occurs with both present and past tenses. The present tense can occur with first person, with certain verbs such as *bāsī-* 'know', with the modal *-dia-*, with the negative *-biri*, and in questions in which the speaker is asking permission. The assumed evidential with past tense is most often used for legends, although the hearsay evidential is also used, especially by the younger generation hearing the stories from older people. Kaye (1970:35–39) has a useful discussion on the assumed evidential which he terms the nonvisible evidential. Examples of the assumed evidential are given in (274)–(278).

(274) ẽrã gɨa wa-kɨ ĩʔã tura-ro   bɨhawere-yũ-bã
     3p 1x go-SR see beˆstrong-DVB beˆsad-ASSUM-3p
     Seeing us leave they probably were very sad (since one is usually sad to see one's friends leave).

(275) Gõãbɨ árĩ-kũ-bĩ   ɨbã-ro-ge
     God   be-ASSUM-3ms beˆhigh-DVB-LOC
     God is on high (in heaven).

(276) suʔri   koe-go   ii-kũ-bõ   pera-ge
     clothes wash-fs do-ASSUM-3fs port-LOC
     She (probably) is washing clothes at the river landing.

(277) bɨ-ya-re   bāsĩ-biri-k-a
     2s-GEN-SPC know-NEG-ASSUM-NON3
     I do not know your language.

(278) bɨʔɨ yoaro-ge aʔhra-y-a
     2s   far-LOC   come-ASSUM-NON3
     You have come a long way (it appears).

The inferred evidential. The speaker using the inferred evidential does not see the event happening but makes an inference about it based on some evidence that he sees. The inferred evidential is composed of a verb phrase with the verb *árĩ-* 'be' acting as an auxiliary suffixed by the recent or remote past marker and verb agreement. There is a certain amount of free fluctuation between this evidential and the assumed. Some Desano speakers feel that the assumed would be used if the event had just happened and the inferred used when referring to it later. Note examples in (279)–(282).

(279) *pisadã wai-re   ba-di-gɨ   árĩ-bĩ*
      cat   fish-SPC eat-PST-ms be-3ms
      The cat must have eaten the fish (you can see his paw marks on the ground where he ate it).

(280) *Boo ɨtãbũ-ge   waʔa wa-di-rã   árĩ-bã*
      Boo rapids-LOC go   go-PST-ANp be-3p
      They must have gone to the Boo rapids (we arrived home and found them absent).

(281) *i   wiʔi   ɨhɨ-di-ro   árĩ-bɨ*
      this house burn-PST-n be-NON3^PST
      This house must have burned (you can see the charred remains).

(282) *Mandu-re   Eduardo paa-di-gɨ árĩ-bĩ*
      Mandu-SPC Edward hit-PST-ms be-3ms
      Edward hit Mandu (you can see the mark where he'd been hit).

Opinion suffix. When -*sõ* is attached to the end of the verb or verb nominalization, it almost always is followed by the speaker saying, 'I think' or 'he thought', and it is about something that hasn't happened or a state of affairs. Examples are given in (283)–(285).

(283) *bãsĩ-yã-bãrĩ-k-a-sõ   árĩ   pepi-pɨ*
      know-PASS-not^be-ASSUM-NON3-opinion say think-HSY^3ms
      It is impossible, he thought.

(284) *Gõãbɨ ya   weredɨ-ri   õã-ri   bãhã   ãʔrã-a-sõ   árĩ*
      God   GEN talk-DVB be^good-DVB PERT be-NON3-opinion say

   pepi-a
   think-NON3^PRES
   God's Word is that which is good, I think.

(285) *õã-gɨ-sõ   yɨ pepi-kɨ baye-tuʔa-ha   dore*
      be^good-ms-opinion 1s think-SR chant-COMPLET-TEL sickness

   tari-gɨkubĩ
   pass-PROB^3ms
   He'll be well, I think. I've finished chanting; he will get over his sickness.

5.3. Tense markers

In addition to the tense evidentials, which reflect whether an event occurred in the past or is happening in the present, Desano distinguishes between remote and recent past and has a three-way system of marking future tense.

Past tense. In the past tense Desano speakers distinguish between remote past and recent past. Recent past is used about events that have just occurred or which occurred during the past week or two, and remote past refers to anything before that. All the evidentials that relate to past events permit this distinction. Recent past is marked by the suffix -a that occurs immediately before the evidential. This suffix is homophonous with or the same as the suffix meaning 'away from the speaker' (§5.6).[18] Remote past is distinguished from the present tense in the visual evidential by the position of stress. There are many morphophonemic changes that occur in the past tense that have to do with -ri+-a becoming -ra, stress, glottal stop, and its relation to stress/pitch (see §§1.15–16).

Examples follow of the present tense and the two types of past tense. In the present tense, (286), the stress/pitch falls on -bĩ; in the recent past, (287), it falls on the recent past marker -a; and, to show remote past, (288), the stress occurs with āsū-.

(286) asū-bĩ́
    buy-3ms
    He buys.

(287) asū-á-bĩ
    buy-REC^PST-3ms
    He bought recently.

(288) āsú-bĩ
    buy-3ms
    He bought.

In examples (289)–(290), wá- 'go' becomes wa?a- in both the present and recent past tenses because the stress/pitch is taken by a different morpheme (see §1.15).

---

[18]Kaye (1970:43–49), in his discussion of the past tense says that this -a *is the same morpheme as the* -a for action away from the speaker.

(289) *waʔa-bḯ*
    go-3ms
    He goes.

(290) *waʔa-á-bĩ̄*
    go-REC͡PST-3ms
    He went (recently).

(291) *wa-bĩ̄*
    go-3ms
    He went.

In examples (292)–(293), *ári-* 'come' has a glottal stop in the present and recent past tenses, and also, in the recent past, the *i* changes to *a* to accommodate the *-a* (recent past marker); in (294) the remote past is indicated by the change in stress.

(292) *aʔri-bḯ*
    come-3ms
    He comes.

(293) *aʔrá-bĩ̄*
    come͡REC͡PST-3ms
    He came (recently).

(294) *ári-bĩ̄*
    come-3ms
    He came.

Future tense. The future tense is formed from the present tense of the assumed evidential and adds additional information about gender, number, and animacy, using the same suffixes that form nominalizations. Although the future tense is in the irrealis mode to indicate that the speaker cannot state with certainty that the event will occur, Desano indicates, by using different markers, how certain or uncertain the speaker is that the event will take place. The table in (295) shows the various future forms in order from least certain to most certain. The least certain uses *-bu/bo* (potential) in place of the gender and number markers in the *boreka* dialect, although the other dialects of Desano place *-bu/bo* just preceding these markers. The future tense in the most

Verb Phrase 71

certain positive mode is used for first person only. The form given in the second column (probably will) is most commonly used.

Some speakers use *-bu...*, *-ko...*, instead of *-bo...*, *-ku....* Vowel harmony also influences the vowels used (§1.16) and some of the suffixes are nasalized from the right (§1.13). Examples of all three modes of future tense are given in (296)–(299).

(295) Future tense markers

	least certain ←————→ most certain		
	might	probably will	future
1ms, 2ms	*-boka*	*-gɨka*	*-gɨra*
1fs, 2fs	*-boka*	*-goka*	*-gora*
1p, 2p	*-boka*	*-rāka*	*-rāra*
3ms	*-bokūbī*	*-gɨkūbī*	
3fs	*-bokūbõ*	*-gokūbõ*	
3p	*-bokōbā*	*-rākōbā*	
NON3	*-boka*	*-roka*	

(296) *yābīgā   deko   ari-boka*
tomorrow water   come-MIGHT^NON3
It may rain tomorrow.

(297) *wɨ-ri-ru   wa-roka   15 de enero   árī-kɨ̃*
fly-DVB-CL go-PROB^NON3 15 of January be-SR
The plane will probably go on the fifteenth of January.

(298) *yɨʔɨ   pepi-a   sīrī-a   wa-gokūbõ*
1s   think-NON3^PRES   die-PERF   go-PROB^3fs
I think she will die.

(299) *gahi   boho-ri-ge   turaro   būkūbiri-ri   bẽrā   wa-gɨra*
other dry-DVB-LOC   much   happy-DVB   with   go-FUT^1ms
Another year I'll go very happily.

Unequivocal (i.e., most certain) negation in the future is expressed with the suffix *-sōbẽ*, as in (300). When this suffix occurs, the verb is not marked for person, number, or gender. When the negation is less certain as in (301), the negative morpheme *-biri* is used with one of the other future tense markers.

(300) *iri-re   ba-sobẽ   ĩgɨ̃*
   this-SPC eat-FUT^NEG 3ms
   He will never eat this.

(301) *ẽrã yãbĩgã   wa-biri-bokõbã*
   3p   tomorrow go-NEG-MIGHT^3p
   Probably they will not go tomorrow.

5.4. Imperative

The imperative suffix replaces the evidential and subject agreement markers in the independent verb. The second-person imperative *-ke* is the most common form used. There are also first- and third-person commands and other forms for second imperative that carry more semantic load than the simple command. The table in (302) presents the imperatives in Desano with both the affirmative and negative forms shown.

(302) Imperative suffixes

First person

permissive (s/p)		*-si*	'Let me/us, May I/we?...'
		-biri-kã-ku-ri	'May we not?...'
		(-NEG-ABS-ASSUM-Q)	
exhortative (p)		*-rã*	'Let's...'
		-biri-kã-rã	'Let's not...'

Second person

direct		*-ke*	'Do...'
		-biri-kã-ke	'Don't...'
courtesy		*-dĩ-sa/ri-sa*	'Go ahead and...'
scolding (NEG)			
	ms	*-bi-ta*	'Don't do...'
	fs	*-bi-go-ta*	'Don't do...'
	ANp	*-bi-rã-ta*	'Don't do...'
permission		*-yã-ta*	'Try...it'

Verb Phrase

warning	-ba	'Be careful that...'
	-bēhē-ba	'Be careful that you don't...'

Third person

indirect (s/p)	-poro	'Let him/her/them/it...'
	-biri-kā-poro	'Don't let...'

Among the second-person imperatives, the direct command is the strongest in both its positive and negative form. In the courtesy form, -dī-sa and -ri-sa seem to be used interchangeably even by the same speaker. This form is composed of -ri/dī, which is the aspect marker meaning 'for now, temporarily', and -sa, which has the meaning of 'at a distance'. This form is used, for example, when visitors arrive in a village hot and tired from a trip. The host tells them to 'go on down and bathe for now; we can talk later'. The composition of the permission form is -yā 'see, try out' and -ta 'limiter' (§11.3). There is limited usage for this form. Each category of the imperative is illustrated in (303)–(311), in the order as listed in the table in (302).

(303) *ĩā-si*
see-PERMISSIVE^IMP
Let me see it! or May I see it?

(304) *guʔa-rã   wa-rã*
bathe-ANp go-HORT^IMP
Let's go bathe!

(305) *yɨ-re   karta   goha-beo-ke*
1s-SPC letter write-send-IMP
Do write and send me a letter!

(306) *guʔa-dī-sa*
bathe-start-distance
Go ahead and bathe for now!

(307) *ii-bi-go-ta*
do-NEG-fs-LIM
Don't do that!

(308) ba-yā-ta
 eat-IMP^prove-LIM
 Eat it to try it out!

(309) yuʔri-bēhē-ba
 fall-NEG-IMP
 Be careful lest you fall!

(310) bɨ̃ā-re o-beo-poro
 2p-SPC give-send-IMP
 Let him send it to you!

(311) ẽrã yābɨ̃gã   ari-biri-kã-poro
 3p tomorrow come-NEG-ABS-IMP
 Don't let them come tomorrow!

Desano has further forms that encode an indirect command to another person which indicates that the speaker wants that person to carry out a certain action. These forms seem to be a more courteous and less direct method of command and are usually in the context of asking a favor. One is the same form used in the main future tense; another is the verb root followed by -bāsɨ̃ (abilitative) (see §5.7); and the third is a verb phrase consisting of verb root plus -kɨ̃ (switch reference) (§10.8) followed by the verb gãʔbẽ/gãbẽ 'want'. Each of these are illustrated in (312)–(314), respectively.

(312) bɨ̃ã wɨ-ri-ru   o-beo-rāka   gɨa poʔro-ge
 2p fly-DVB-CL give-send-PROB^NON3 1x   near-LOC
 You will send the plane to our location (send the plane!).

(313) bɨ̃ã ɨ̃gɨ̃-re   karta   goha-bāsɨ̃-a
 2s   3ms-SPC letter write-ABIL-NON3^PRES
 You can write him a letter (write a letter!).

(314) bɨ̃ã gɨa-re oko   o-beo-kɨ̃   gãʔbẽ-a
 2s   1x-SPC medicine give-send-SR want-NON3^PRES
 I want you to send us medicine.

Desano has a deontic compound verb that is commonly used in hortatory and procedural discourse. This construction consists of the verb root plus -ro (neuter gender) followed by the verb gãʔbẽ/gãbẽ 'want' plus -a/bɨ (non-third person, present/past). Other suffixes can occur between the verb

Verb Phrase

root and -ro. This deontic verb phrase is an impersonal construction. The verb root followed by -ro acts as the subject of the auxiliary verb which agrees with this inanimate subject. The agent or understood subject, most frequently bārī (we inclusive), is the indirect object, not obligatorily marked or stated, as seen in examples (315)–(317).

(315) sabado   árī-kɨ   bõʔbẽ-ro   gãʔbẽ-a-bɨ
      Saturday be-SR work-n   want-REC^PST-NON3^PST
      When it was Saturday, it was necessary to work.

(316) ẽrã bẽrã wai wẽhẽ-ro gãʔbẽ-a
      3p   with fish kill-n   want-NON3^PRES
      We should fish with them (worms).

(317) ẽrã ya-sã-re   sẽrẽ-basa-ro gãʔbẽ-a   bārī-re
      3p   GEN-also-SPC ask-BEN-n   want-NON3^PRES 1i-SPC
      We/One should ask on their behalf also.

A common occurrence with this construction is the nominalized verb phrase erop-ii-gɨ 'thus-do-ms' (therefore). It may occur by itself, as in example (318), or with bārī (we inclusive) as in example (319). The masculine singular ending on this expression does not agree with the neuter marking on the main verb or the plural status of the understood subject bārī.

(318) erop-ii-gɨ   õã-ro   ɨ̃ã-bã   wa-ro   gãʔbẽ-a
      thus-DO-ms   be^good-DVB see-quickly   go-n   want-NON3^PRES
      Therefore, one should watch carefully (seeing quickly) as he goes.

(319) bārī erop-ii-gɨ   Gõãbɨ-re   ũbũpeo-ro   gãʔbẽ-a
      1i   thus-DO-ms   God-SPC   believe-n   want-NON3^PRES
      We/One therefore should believe in God.

When the understood subject or agent is in another person, a less common occurrence, then the subject must be stated and marked with the case marker -re, as in (320).

(320) ɨ̃gɨ-re   wa-ro   gãʔbẽ-a
      3ms-SPC   go-n   want-NON3^PRES
      He must go.

5.5. Aspectuals

The aspects of progressive and perfect are indicated by verb phrases; other aspects are indicated by suffixes that follow the verb root and precede the evidential or the subordinate verb suffix.

The progressive aspect is formed by a main verb stem with suffixes that indicate gender, number, and animacy, plus the auxiliary verb -*ii* 'do', followed by one of the evidentials. This progressive aspect construction occurs in all three tenses and with any evidentials. Appropriate aspectual and modal suffixes can occur with the progressive on both the main and auxiliary verbs. The auxiliary verb *ii-* 'do' occurs also as an independent verb root. Examples using the verb *ba-* 'eat' with various evidentials illustrate the present progressive in (321)–(322), the past progressive in (323)–(324), and the future progressive in (325)–(326).

(321) *ba-go ii-bõ*
 eat-fs do-3fs
 She is eating.

(322) *ba-go ii-kũ-bõ*
 eat-fs do-ASSUM-3fs
 She is eating (assumed).

(323) *ba-go ii-a-bõ*
 eat-fs do-REC^PST-3fs
 She was eating (recent past).

(324) *ba-go ii-a-po*
 eat-fs do-REC^PST-HSY^3fs
 She was eating (recent past hearsay).

(325) *ba-go ii-gokũbõ*
 eat-fs do-PROB^3fs
 She is going to eat.

(326) *ba-bu-go ii-bõ*
 eat-POT-fs do-3fs
 She is about to eat (but may not; see §5.7).

The perfect aspect is coded by the verb root plus the suffix -*a* (perfect) followed by *wa-* 'go' acting as an auxiliary verb, as in (327). Other suffixes can occur between the verb root and -*a* as shown in (328).

Verb Phrase

(327) Ñu   sĩrĩ-a   wa-bĩ
     John   die-PERF   go-3ms
     John has died.

(328) ĩgɨ   tua-kɨ   diaye dɨrɨ-biri-a   wa-yũ-bĩ
      3ms   attach-SR dog   follow-NEG-PERF   go-ASSUM-3ms
      Since he (the tick) attached, the dog has no longer gone after other animals.

The suffixes listed in (329) follow the verb root and precede the evidential or the subordinate verb suffix to indicate other aspects. Many of these suffixes are also verb roots that can occur alone, usually with a slightly different meaning, so could be interpreted as compounds (§5.10). However, since they are highly productive, they are considered to be aspects. Their verb root meaning is given in the third column. Following the list of aspects in (329) are illustrations of each suffix (bolded), in corresponding order with the list, in examples (330)–(347).

(329) Aspectual suffixes

-a	perfect	
-bã	action done quickly or in a hurry	probably comes from the verb õbã- 'run'
-du?u	leave off doing	du?u- 'leave off doing'
-gã	action occurs with movement from one spot to another	derived from wã?gã- 'get up'; some still use the full form
-ha	telic	
-bɨ?tã	do first	bɨ?tã- 'go first'
-bɨrĩ	habitual	
-dēbõ	additive	dēbõ- 'do more'
-dĩ/ri	temporarily, afterward something else will happen	
-dĩgĩ	continuative	dĩgĩ- 'stand'
-dũgũ	action done to an object and object stays in that state	comes from dũgũ- 'stand something'
-dɨgã	inceptive	dɨgã- 'begin'

-dɨ̃rɨ̃	durative	dɨ̃rɨ̵- 'follow after'
-pe?o	totality	pe?o- 'complete'; the action is transitive which means the action is completed on an object
-pe?re	totality	pe?re- 'be complete/finished off', i.e., subject is complete
-tu?a	completive	tu?a- 'finish an action'
-wea	do all in a single action	
-yu	do in anticipation	

(330) *wa?a-a   wa-bã*
go-PERF go-3p
They have gone!

(331) *bã-ge   wa-rã   doa-bã-gã-rãka*
trail-LOC go-ANp sit-quickly-MOVE-PROBˆ1p
While going along the trail, we will sit down for short times as we hurry along.

(332) *bõ?bẽ-du?u-ke*
work-leaveˆoff-IMP
Leave off working!

(333) *bari-re   aɨ̃-gã-ke*
food-SPC take-MOVE-IMP
Take the food (to another spot)!

(334) *bẽrẽ-ha-bĩ*
fall-TEL-3ms
He fell to the ground.

(335) *bɨ̃-pɨ   wa-bɨ̃?tã-ke*
2s-FOC go-first-IMP
You go first!

(336) ērā-re presu ii-**bīrī** bia-dobo-**bīrī** wēhē-**bīrī** ii-yū-bā
3p-SPC prison do-HAB shut-set-HAB kill-HAB do-ASSUM-3p
They habitually put them in prison, shut them up (in prison), and killed them.

(337) yābīka árī-kɨ bõʔbẽ-**dẽbõ**-bā
afternoon be-SR work-ADDITIVE-3p
In the afternoon they work more.

(338) deko piu-**dī**-ha-bõ
water pour-start-TEL-3fs
She pours in water gradually.

(339) ba-**dīgī**-kā-bā
eat-CONTIN-ABS-3p
They continually ate.

(340) ɨ̃gɨ̃ ya poreru piʔri-**dūgū**-kā-pɨ
3ms GEN tail leave^off-stand-ABS-HSY^3ms
He left his tail lying there.

(341) ẽrā dõbẽ pee bāsī-**dɨgā**-ha-yõ-rā
3p women hear know-begin-TEL-HSY-3p
These women finally began to understand.

(342) paa-**dīrī**-kā-pɨ
hit-DURATIVE-ABS-HSY^3ms
He kept on hitting him.

(343) poe-ri opa-rā opa-**peʔo**-kā-a bārī
field-p have-ANp have-TOTAL-ABS-NON3^PRES 1i
If we have fields, we have everything (we need).

(344) era-**peʔre**-kā-bā
arrive-TOTAL-ABS-3p
They all arrived.

(345) ba-**tuʔa**-ha-bɨ yɨʔɨ
eat-COMPLET-TEL-NON3^PST 1s
I have finished eating.

(346) *deko-re   pi-**wea**-ke*
water-SPC pour-do^all-IMP
Pour out all the water!

(347) *õ-ge   árĩ-**yu**-ke*
here-LOC be-anticipation-IMP
Stay here in anticipation (of our arrival)!

5.6. Directionals

The morphology of the directional formatives, or deictic markers, suggests that they are derived from the verbs *wa-* 'go' and *ari-* 'come'. The usual affix to indicate action away from the speaker is *-a* (348) and towards speaker is *-ri* (present) (349) or *-ra-* (*-ri* + *-a* past) (350).

(348) *i   wiʔi-ge   bāhā-a-dɨgā-yõ-rā   daha*
this house-LOC go^up-away-begin-HSY-3p again
They went up to the house again (away from the speaker).

(349) *erop-ii   bɨrĩ-ri-yõ-rā   daha*
thus-do go^up-toward-HSY-3p again
They continued traveling upriver (towards the speaker).

(350) *Mandu buʔa-ra   ii-bĩ   Manuel ya   wiʔi-ge*
Mandu go^down-towards^PST do-3ms Manuel GEN house-LOC
Mandu came down to Manuel's house.

The directional suffixes can be attached to any of the directional verbs (§2.2).

(351) *Viviano bāhā-ra-bĩ   wiʔi-ge*
Viviano go^up-toward^PST-3ms house-LOC
Viviano went up to the house (towards the speaker).

When these suffixes occur with *duha* 'remain at one's base', they indicate returning to one's base.

(352) *duha-ri-ke   duru*
remain-toward-IMP quickly
Return quickly (towards the speaker)!

(353) duha-a-ke   duru
    remain-away-IMP quickly
    Return quickly (away from the speaker)!

Another directional suffix is -*bia* (omnilocative), noted by Kaye (1970:71). It has a limited distribution.

(354) *ĩgɨ*   *ĩã-bia-peho-kã-bĩ*
    3ms   see-OMNILOCATIVE-TOTAL-ABS-3ms
    He saw everything.

(355) *Bogotá-ge*   *kuri-bia-kã-bõ*
    Bogotá-LOC   travel-OMNILOCATIVE-ABS-3fs
    She visited all of Bogotá.

5.7. Modal suffixes

The potential, dubitative, frustrative, desiderative, and abilitative moods are coded by a series of verbal suffixes that follow the verb root and precede the evidentials. They can be subdivided as being epistemic (absolute truth value) or deontic (participant volition); (Palmer 1986:18). Kaye (1970:50–51) brings out a difference between the evidential and the mood system that, given an event, a speaker is constrained to choose one and only one member of the evidential system, whereas the speaker may or may not mark his certainty about the event with a modal. The modal suffixes are given in (356).[19]

(356) Modal suffixes

	Epistemic		Deontic	
potential	dubitative	frustrative	desiderative	abilitative
-*bu/bo* (POT)	-*sa* -*sia*	-*ri*/-*ra*	-*dia*	-*bãsĩ*

The POTENTIAL SUFFIX -*bu/bo* has the meaning of 'about to'. Another way of expressing it is that, given the facts, the event should occur but may not. The variation in form is due to vowel harmony (§1.16).

---

[19] Kaye (1970:54–55) terms -*bo* a dubitative. Also, contrary to my findings, he describes -*ri* (-*di*) as an assertive, which "indicates an event that the speaker asserts took place, usually in the face of apparently contrary evidence" (p. 52). I also do not agree with his equating the past nominative marker -*di* with the "assertive" marker (p. 53).

Example (357) is in the progressive aspect (§5.5). (See §5.3 for the use of -*bu/bo* in connection with the least certain future marker 'might'. See also §10.3 for its use in nominalizations and §10.8 in the contrafactual clause.)

(357) bari   bõã-bo   ii-bõ
      food   prepare-POT   do-3fs
      She is about to prepare the food.

The DUBITATIVE SUFFIXES are used when the Desano speaker not only wants to indicate whether or not he has seen the event by using evidentials, but also to indicate that he isn't sure of his information; -*sa* 'doubt' occurs most often with the assumed evidential. Examples (358)–(359) compare the meanings between the use of the present assumed evidential alone and with the addition of -*sa*.

(358) wiʔi-ge   árĩ-kũ-bõ
      house-LOC   be-ASSUM-3fs
      She is in the house. (I know she is there but I don't see her.)

(359) wiʔi-ge   árĩ-sa-kũ-bõ
      house-LOC   be-doubt-ASSUM-3fs
      She may be in the house; I don't know for sure.

The suffix -*sa* is most frequently used with the first person assumed evidential to indicate that the speaker is trying to recall something, as in (360).

(360) doʔpa   ãrĩ-sa-k-a
      what   say-doubt-ASSUM-NON3^PRES
      What was it I said now?

The suffix -*sia* indicates less doubt than -*sa* and occurs with the visual evidential, as the speaker has some kind of visual or oral clue that leads him to believe in the truth of his assertion. In (361), for example, he may see a door open or hear a sound inside that leads him to believe that the person is at home.

(361) wiʔi-ge   árĩ-sia-bõ
      house-LOC   be-doubt-3fs
      She seems to be in the house.

The FRUSTRATIVE SUFFIX *-ri* indicates that the purpose of the event was not accomplished, as in (362). In the past, *-ra* (*-ri* + *-a* §1.16) is used as in (363).

(362) bākā-ge   eha-ri-bɨ
      town-LOC arrive-FRUST-NON3^PST
      I arrived at the town (but I didn't accomplish what I went there for).

(363) kobē-soro-ri bērā deko   kóā-ra-bɨ
      metal-pot-p   with water throw^away-FRUST^PST-NON3^PST
      We threw out the water (from the hole) with pots (but we didn't get the water all out).

The DESIDERATIVE SUFFIX *-dia* is illustrated in (364), and example (365) illustrates the combination of the desiderative (on the main verb) and the frustrative (on the auxiliary).

(364) bɨā-re   i   kere   were-dia-k-a
      2p-SPC this news   say-DESID-ASSUM-NON3
      I want to tell you this news.

(365) Alfonso gahi-gɨ   ari-dia-di-gɨ   árī-ra-bī
      Alfonso other-ms   come-DESID-PST-ms   be-FRUST-3ms
      Alfonso was another one who had wanted to come (but didn't make it).

The ABILITATIVE SUFFIX *-bāsī* is from the verb root 'know'. When used as a modal suffix, it is an abilitative as in (366). Examples (367)–(368) show the difference in meaning when *bāsī-* occurs as a separate verb root with a medial clause from when it occurs as the abilitative modal suffix.

(366) īgɨ   īgɨ   yīgɨ wa-bāsī-biri-di-gɨ   wa-bāsī-yū-bī
      3ms   3ms(GEN)   leg   go-ABIL-NEG-PST-ms   go-ABIL-ASSUM-3ms
      The one who was not able to walk could now walk.

(367) igo-re   ī?ā   bāsī-bā
      3fs-SPC see   know-3p
      They identified her.

(368) *igo-re   ĩã-bãsĩ-bã*
3fs-SPC see-ABIL-3p
They could see her.

Some modal and aspectual suffixes can vary in their order following the verb root without change of meaning, as in (369) and (370).

(369) *ba-dia-bɨrĩ-dēbõ-bĩ*   or   *ba-dēbõ-bɨrĩ-dia-bĩ*
eat-DESID-HAB-more-3ms   eat-more-HAB-DESID-3ms
He always wanted to eat more.

(370) *ii-peʔo-dēbõ-bãsĩ-biri-bɨrĩ-pɨ*
do-TOTAL-more-ABIL-NEG-HAB-HSY^3ms
    or
ii-peʔo-dēbõ-biri-bãsĩ-bɨrĩ-pɨ
do-TOTAL-more-NEG-ABIL-HAB-HSY^3ms
    or
ii-dēbõ-peʔo-bãsĩ-biri-bɨrĩ-pɨ
do-more-TOTAL-ABIL-NEG-HAB-HSY^3ms
He never could do it all. (The Desano speaker felt the third utterance was most natural).

5.8. Miscellaneous suffixes

This section discusses other notions which are expressed in the verb and verb phrase by suffixes that follow the verb root and precede the evidential marker. They tend to occur right after the verb that they modify or after the directional suffixes, then can be followed by the aspect and modal suffixes and the emphasizer *-kã* (see examples (378) and (380)).

AUGMENTATIVE INTENSITY is expressed by the suffixes *-tari*, *-pũrĩ*, and *-goʔra*. *-tari* is considered to indicate the strongest intensity and is the most productive, followed by *-pũrĩ*. *-goʔra* has more the idea of 'actually or exactly'. *purĩ-* and *tari-* are also verb roots meaning 'pass' and 'hurt' respectively. For a discussion of *goʔra* used as a definer of a noun, see §3.11.

(371) *asi-pũrĩ-kara-bɨ*
be^hot-INTEN-seem-NON3^PST
It was very hot.

Verb Phrase

(372) *iri-re   gābẽ-tari-k-a*
　　　this-SPC want-INTEN-ASSUM-NON3
　　　I want this very much.

(373) *yɨ-pɨ   bẽrẽ-go?ra-biri-bɨ*
　　　1s-FOC beˆdrunk-INTEN-NEG-NON3ˆPST
　　　I actually did not get drunk.

Two suffixes encode MITIGATION (the opposite of intensity). They are *-yārī* 'a little' and *-keya* 'almost' as in (374)–(375). Like *go?ra*, these suffixes can also attach to other parts of speech as in (376).

(374) *ōā-yārī-ro   yɨ?ɨ pepi-a   pare*
　　　beˆgood-DIMINISHER-DVB 1s   think-NON3ˆPRES finally
　　　I am feeling a little better finally.

(375) *ōā-keya-bī*
　　　beˆgood-DIMINISHER-3ms
　　　He is almost better.

(376) *pɨ?rɨ-yāri   wa-rāka*
　　　after-DIMINISHER go-PROBˆNON3ˆANp
　　　We'll go in a little while.

The suffix *-po* encodes the meaning of 'accustom to' as in (377).

(377) *yapi-gɨ   árī-gɨ-sā   ōā-ro   árī-po-a*
　　　beˆfull-ms   be-ms-also   beˆgood-DVB   be-accustom-PERF

　　　wa-k-a
　　　go-ASSUM-NON3ˆPRES
　　　I have accustomed myself also to being full.

The suffix *-bāa* seems to encode the idea of doing an action foolishly, without planning, accidentally; the suffix *-kā* 'absolutely' makes an assertion more comprehensive. Both of these occur in (378).

(378) *eropa ārī-bāa-kā-biri-bu-y-a*
　　　thus   say-fool-ABS-NEG-POT-ASSUM-NON3
　　　I wouldn't just be talking into the air (like an absolute fool).

Some time suffixes are *-dẽã* 'all day' and *-botabũ* 'all night'. Their morphology seems to indicate that they are more than a suffix, but they are bound to the verb root; *-botabũ* seems to come from *boyo-tabũ* (dawn-help) 'help the dawn'.

(379) *baya-botabũ-a-pɨ*
dance-all^night-PERF-HSY^3ms
He has danced all night.

(380) *árĩ-dẽã-kã-bã*
be-all^day-ABS-3p
They were around absolutely all day.

The suffix *-gua* 'do as a habit' is used in the sense of talking about whether or not that person will do an action and saying he probably will because he customarily does it. (The *-ba* in the context of (382) probably comes from the interjection of doubt *ũba*. See §2.5.)

(381) *soo-ri-dɨ   árĩ-kɨ wi?i-ge   árĩ-gua-bĩ*
rest-DVB-day be-SR house-LOC be-habit-3ms
On Sunday he should be at his house as he usually is.

(382) *wa-gua-bĩ-ba   gahi-subu-re*
go-habit-3ms-uncertainty other-time-SPC
Perhaps he'll go this time since he regularly does other times.

The suffix *-sɨa* has the meaning of 'like, enjoy, it pleases'. It can occur alone, also, with about the same meaning.

(383) *ba-sɨa-bĩ*
eat-enjoy-3ms
He likes to eat.

The suffix *-tura-* 'be strong' is included in this list of miscellaneous suffixes because it can follow almost any verb giving the meaning of 'do with strength'.

(384) *kãrĩ-tura-bĩ*
sleep-be^strong-3ms
He sleeps a lot.

(385) gūyá-tura-bĩ
 think-beˆstrong-3ms
 He is not frightened/has faith.

(386) baya-tura-bĩ
 sing-beˆstrong-3ms
 He sings in a loud voice.

(387) doa-tura-bĩ
 sit-beˆstrong-3ms
 He doesn't get tired sitting.

5.9. Auxiliary verbs

Desano has two auxiliary verbs, *ii-* 'do' and *wa-* 'go'.

ii- 'do' occurs as an auxiliary in three different types of verb phrase. The first one forms the progressive aspect as described in §5.5 and is illustrated in (388).

(388) ba-go ii-bõ
 eat-fs do-3fs
 She is eating.

In the second type, *ii-* carries the main verb markers for a series of one or more medial clauses (see §10.8) as in (389). It appears that the function of marking events with the auxiliary *ii-* is to background them in the narrative. Example (390) is from a travelogue that included a study course. Nontravel and nonstudying events are marked with *ii-*.

(389) iri wiʔi-ge eha gahi-dõ-re-ta weretabũ ii-bɨ
 that house-LOC arrive other-CL-SPC-LIM discuss do-NON3ˆPST
 Arriving at that house, we discussed other things.

(390) erop-ii-gɨ   Taraboagoro-ge   eha   gɨa   ya   wiʔi-ge
      thus-do-ms   Taraboagoro-LOC   arrive   1x   GEN   house-LOC

   bāhā-a   yaʔa-re   ābū   ii-bɨ
   goˆupˆawayˆfrom   1sˆGEN-SPC   arrange   do-NON3ˆPST

   erop-ii-gɨ   iri   yābɨ-re   ero-ta   kārī   soo-ri-dɨ
   thus-do-ms   this   night-SPC   there-LIM   sleep   rest-DVB-day

   árī-kɨ-re   yābɨ-yārī-gā   wiri-bɨ   pare
   be-SR-SPC   night-DIMIN-DIM   leave-NON3ˆPST   finally

   And so, I arrived at Taraboagoro, went up to our house and arranged my things. Then that night I slept there, and on Sunday very early in the morning I left, finally.

The third type is the analytical causative described in §6.1.

The verb *wa-* 'go' functions as an auxiliary verb to form the perfect aspect as in (391); see §5.5:

(391) Ñu   sīrī-a   wa-bī
      John   die-PERF   go-3ms
      John has died.

5.10–5.12 Verb compounding

Desano makes use of verb compounding to enrich and expand the meaning of a clause. When two or more independent roots form a verb compound, they can be distinguished from two medial clauses by their occurring with one stress which distinguishes one word, and by nothing coming between the roots, except at times a bound verb root such as *-bēʔ-* 'throw, do with force' as in (392).

(392) ĩa-bēʔ-būhū-bī
      see-throw-causeˆtoˆascend-3ms
      He looked up with head back.

In text, not more than four verb roots have been found compounded, but in solicited data five verbs could be combined. Verb roots that follow the first root are often contracted. For example, the verb *api-* 'place' becomes *-pi* when it follows other verb roots as shown in (393).

(393) aī-būhū-pi   wiʔi-ge
      carry-cause^to^go^up-place   house-LOC
      Carrying (it) up and putting (it) in the house...

When verbs form a compound, one verb in the compound could be called the head verb and the other(s) the modifying verb(s). In (393) above *aī-* 'carry' would be the head verb.

Desano has many bound affixes that could be called either derivational affixes or dependent verb roots that can only occur combined with another verb root to form a stem.[20] These bound affixes appear to be derived from independent stems and should be considered as bound verb roots. Some of them, like *pi-* 'pour a liquid', are more like the main verb and need another verb to modify them. Most of them, however, combine with the main verb to modify it. Some of these occur only preceding the head verb, or can occur both preceding or following, or only follow. For example, the affix *bō?-*, indicating that the verb action is done with the fingers or hand, occurs only preceding another verb; *-bē?-* 'throwing motion or force' can occur preceding or following another verb.

Of the many aspectual and modal suffixes which occur following the main verb, many are independent verb roots. Most of the remaining are probably historically verb roots that now cannot occur alone. The distinction between verb compounding and the aspectual, modal, directional, and miscellaneous suffixes or roots is their distribution. The aspectual, modal, and directional roots can potentially modify any verb, whereas the verbs in compounds can only occur with a limited set of roots. Also, the verbs in compounds are generally directly attached to each other, while some of the other suffixes or roots can move around in the verb phrase (§5.8).

Aspectual, modal, directional, and other verb modifiers have been discussed in §§5.5–5.8. Sections 5.10–5.12 give examples of independent verb roots and bound verb roots that compound with some verbs to modify them. Many of these are directional verbs such as *bāhā-* 'ascend' or *būhū-* 'cause to ascend'. Others of these carry the main meaning of the phrase. There are also examples of several independent verb roots that commonly form compounds, besides those that are seen occurring

---

[20] Jacobsen points out (Macaulay 1993:70), when discussing Washo verb stem structure, that: "it is likely that the elements that are synchronically prefixes are diachronically derived from independent stems. This former independence of the prefixes is suggested especially by the concreteness of their meanings and by their categorization into intransitive and transitive types."

with the bound roots. Section §5.13 discusses noun incorporation, another form of compounding.

5.10. Bound verb roots that modify the main verb

Bound verb roots are always followed by an aspectual suffix or preceded or followed by another root. This section lists common compounds involving a bound verb root which modifies the main verb.

The suffix *bõʔ-* has the meaning of doing with one's hands plus, in some cases, the added meaning of turning over; *bõʔbẽ-* 'work' also has the meaning of 'hand' when in a compound. It is compared with *bõʔ-* in example (394). In some cases it does not occur in the same compound as *bõʔ-*, but in others it does with a different meaning.

(394) *bõʔ-pi-*   hand-place^on^ground
                      'turn over something with one's hands so that it is upside down'

    bõʔ-bāhĩ-pi-   hand-turn^over-place
                      'turn back over so that it is right side up', e.g., a canoe

    bõʔbẽ-pi-   work-place
                      'touch with one's whole hand'

    bõʔbẽ-pi-yã   touch-place-check^out
                      'touch with one's hand to find out something'

    bõʔ-yēā-   hand-grab
                      'touch, squeeze with one's fingers and hand'

    bõhõtõ bõʔ-siu- hand hand-hang
                      'spread one's hands out'

    bõʔ-siu-   hand-hang
                      'hang something upside down' (cf. with *duʔ-siu* 'hang over something')

    bõʔ-tu-   hand-put^against
                      'put against something the other way around or so it is partially upside down'

Verb Phrase

bõʔbẽ-tuu-	hand-push	'pull the trigger on a gun'
bõʔ-baã-	hand-foolishly	'feel around without seeing'
bõʔ-būtū-	hand-crumble	'crumble into powder with one's fingers'
bõʔ-siri-dihu-	hand-scatter-cause^to^descend	'crumble over the floor or ground'
bõʔ-dōhẽa-	hand-twist	'twist' (cf. pūgɨ dōhea 'roll up a hammock')
bõʔ-yɨsɨ-a-	hand-bundle-VB	'make into a bundle'
bõʔ-tɨã-	hand-squeeze	'squeeze something with one's fingers so that it breaks open', e.g., breaking an egg
bõʔ-diu-	hand-put^pressure^on	'put pressure on with one's fingers'
bõʔ-dobo	hand-set	'set upside down'

The suffix yā- seems to be related to yēā- 'grab'; yā- describes an action performed more with the whole hand or palm, whereas bõʔ- is more with the fingers. (Both yātɨã and bõʔtɨã may be used with the meaning 'squeeze/pop with fingers to cause liquid to come out', e.g., 'squeeze/pop a bee between one's fingers to kill it'.) Compounds with yā- are listed in (395).

(395) yā-būtū-   palm-crumble
'crumble something by putting it under something else then rub against it or with the palm of one's hand'

	yã-tu-	palm-put^against 'put palm of the hand or something else against something', e.g., against a wall
	yã-peo	palm-place^on^something 'place palm of the hand or something else lightly on another object'
	yã-diu-	palm-put^pressure^on 'put pressure on with the palm of one's hand'
	yã-pu-	palm-inject 'poke at with something sharp in one's fist'
	yã-tĩã-	palm-squeeze 'break open using something else, with one's fist around the other item'

(396) *kɨʔra-* 'action done with one's feet/step'

kɨʔra-tĩã-	step-squeeze 'step on something hard so that it breaks open'
kɨʔra-pi-	step-place^on^the^ground 'step on the ground'
kɨʔra-tu-	step-put^against 'put one's foot against something else'
kɨʔra-peo-	step-place^on^something 'put one's foot on top of something else'
kɨʔra-dihu-	step-cause^to^descend 'push something downward with one's foot'
kɨʔra-biʔa-	step-close 'close something with one's foot'
kɨʔra-diu-	step-put^pressure^on 'put pressure with one's foot'

Verb Phrase

	kɨʔra-pea-	step-break
		'break with one's foot'
	kɨʔra-ta-	step-cut
		'step on something causing one's foot to be cut'

(397) *bẽʔ-* 'throw or do with force'

	bẽʔ-pi-	throw-place ̂on ̂the ̂ground
		'throw down to the ground'
	bẽʔ-bũhũ-	throw-cause ̂to ̂ascend
		'throw up into the air'
	bẽʔ-dihu-	throw-cause ̂to ̂descend
		'throw down'
	bẽʔ-yuu-	throw-send ̂downriver
		'throw into water so it goes downriver'
	bẽʔ-tu-	throw-put ̂against
		'throw against something'
	bẽʔ-beha-	throw-settle ̂on
		'throw with force on top of something else'
	bẽʔ-biʔa-	force-close
		'get stuck in mud'
	bẽʔ-dũa-	throw-break
		'throw, cause to break in two'
	bẽʔ-dũgũ-	force-cause ̂to ̂stand
		'pound with an upright object like a tree'
	bẽʔ-pa-	force-float ̂on ̂water
		'land with a splash on the water'
	bẽʔ-pu-a-	throw-inject-PERF
		'put into something with force', e.g., throwing darts

	bẽʔ-bẽre-ha-	force-goˆdown-TEL 'fall down hard'
	bẽʔ-ta-	force-cut 'hit against something and get cut'
	bẽʔ-uhu-	force-scrape 'hit against and scrape one's skin on something'
	bẽʔ-sã-	throw-enter 'throw with force to enter', e.g., a basket in a hoop
	bẽʔ-peo-	throw-placeˆonˆsomething 'drop onto something else'
	bẽʔ-tuʔa-ha-	force-finish-TEL 'hit against something hard' as in (398)

(398) ĩbĩka   bẽʔ-tuʔa-ha-a   bũhĩ-re
     smoke force-COMPLET-TEL-NON3ˆPRES leaves-SPC
     Smoke from a big fire hits against the roof.

If *bẽʔ-* is removed from (398), the meaning is that the fire is almost out and the smoke goes gently against the roof.

When the suffix *bẽʔ-* is in the middle of a verb compound, the glottal is dropped. Note the list in (399).

(399)
	tuu-bẽ-aku-	push-force-putˆinto 'shove into', e.g., a hole
	tuu-bẽ-sã	push-force-putˆinto 'give something a push so it goes into something, like a pot in water'
	tuu-bẽ-tu	push-force-putˆagainst 'give something a hard push against something else'
	gasiru duʔ-bẽ-yu-	canoe loosen-throw-sendˆdownriver 'give a boat a push to get it off shore to go downriver'

Verb Phrase

pee-bẽ-dihu-	hear-force-causeˆtoˆdescend	
	'listen hard to capture a sound below'	
pee-bẽ-bũhũ-	hear-force-causeˆtoˆascend	
	'listen hard to capture a sound above'	
puri-bẽ-bũhũ-	blow-force-causeˆtoˆascend	
	'blow hard above'	
ĩʔã-bẽ-bũhũ-	see-force-causeˆtoˆascend	
	'look up with one's head back'	
tuu-bẽ-wiu-	push-force-causeˆtoˆleave	
	'throw something outside'	
o-bẽ-dihu-	give-force/throw-causeˆtoˆdescend	
	'throw down gently' (cf. with *bẽʔ-dihu-* 'throw down hard')	

The form *-diu* 'put pressure on' may function as a main verb as *bõʔ-diu* 'put pressure on with one's fingers' in (394), or as a modifier as listed in (400).

(400) *peo-diu-* placeˆonˆtopˆof-pressure
  'hold something down', e.g., put something on top of something else so the wind doesn't carry it away

  doa-diu- sit-pressure
  'sit on something with pressure'

  dɨgĩ-diu- stand-pressure
  'stand on something with pressure'

  ii-diu do-pressure
  'do with pressure'

  yẽʔã-diu- grab-pressure
  'hold onto something hard'

(401) *pu-a-* inject-PERF, *pu-* 'inject' is an independent verb

    bui-pu-a-   shoot^arrow-inject-PERF
                'shoot an arrow into something'

    dea-pu-a- throw-inject-PERF
                'throw a machete, etc., into something, e.g., the ground'

    yõsẽ-pu-a- spear-inject-PERF
                'spear into something'

    bẽʔ-pu-a- throw-inject-PERF
                'play darts'

(402) *yuʔa-* 'move backwards with one's head going back'

    yuʔa-ha-bẽrẽ- backwards-TEL-go^down
                    'fall on one's back (accidentally)'

    yuʔa-bẽre-ha- backwards-go^down-TEL
                    'fall on one's back without an accidental component'

    yuʔa-diha- backwards-go^straight^down
                'go down on one's back'

    koʔre-yua- trip-backwards
                'trip so one's head jerks backward'

    yuʔa-yã-bũhũ- backwards-see-cause^to^ascend
                  'put one's head back to take a look up' as in (403)

(403) *koʔre-gɨ yuʔa-bũhũ-a-bĩ*
     trip-ms head^back-cause^to^ascend-REC^PST-3ms
     He tripped and his head fell back.

    The form *beha-* 'settle on' modifies the verb to which it is attached; in several cases it combines with several of the bound verb roots above

Verb Phrase

that also have a modifying function. It does not occur first in the compound.[21] Some of its compounds are listed in (404).

(404) kɨʔra-beha- step-settleˆon
  'put one's feet on top of something'

  yā-beha grab-settleˆon
   'grab while on top of'

  bẽʔ-beha- force-settleˆon
   'do with force on top of something else'

  bɨrī-beha ascend-settleˆon
   'go up and settle on something', e.g., a bird in a tree

  cārī-beha sleep-settleˆon
   'sleep on top of something'

  wiri-beha- leave-settleˆon
   'leave a place and settle on something', e.g., a bee leaving its nest and perching on top of it

  āī-beha carry-settleˆon
   'carrying something, settle on top of something'

5.11. Bound verb roots that function as a main verb

Two such bound verb roots are listed in (405), with illustrations in context in (406)–(407); others are listed in (408)–(411).

---

[21] *beha-* also occurs productively following a verb root plus the neuter gender *-ro* to give the meaning of 'feel like doing', which most often occurs with the negative. Another form of *beha-* means 'appear', which is often used in a construction like *igo pago dopa beha-bō* 'she looks like her mother.'

(405) *duʔkua-* 'bend something that can bend like a joint'

    aĩ-duʔkua-   carry-bend
                            'kneel'

    bōhōtōre aĩ-duʔkua-   hand carry-bend
                                      'bend elbow'

ore-/oʔre- 'loosen'

    oʔre-pore-   loosen-expand
                         'explode'

(406) *ore-bāā-diha-k-a*
loosen-accidental-descend-ASSUM-NON3^PRES
It falls without planning through a hole in the roof or into a hole in the ground while standing there.

(407) *yese-a ore-wiri-a-bā*
pig-p loosen-leave-PERF-3p
The pigs made an opening in the fence and got out.

(408) *pi-* 'pour a liquid'

    pi-u-   pour-do^carefully
               'pour carefully into', like drops into an eye (-*u* does not have independent meaning)

    pi-sã-   pour-put^into
               'pour into something'

    pi-pi-   pour-place^on^the^ground
               'pour liquid onto the ground'

    pi-beo-   pour-throw
                'pour/throw liquid'

    pi-kóã-   pour-throw^away
                'throw out liquid'

Verb Phrase

pi-dihu-   pour-cause^to^descend
'pour/throw liquid downwards'

pi-bẽ-bũhũ-   pour-force-cause^to^ascend
'pour/throw liquid upwards real high' (this construction needs the addition of *bẽ-* 'force')

pi-aku-   pour-put^inside
'pour into a closed container'

(409) *po?-* 'pour/put a solid from a container to something else', can occur with the same roots that *pi-* does, such as:

po?-sã-   'pour/put into something'

(410) *-pore-* 'multiply, expand'

kõyõ-pore-   warm-expand
'exude warmth'

ore-pore-   loosen-expand
'explode'

(411) *yuri-* 'go downriver' has the meaning of 'fall' when combined with other verb roots.

yuri-bẽrẽ-ha-   fall-go^down-TEL
'fall from a standing position'

yuri-diha-   fall-descend
'fall from a height'

Components of verb roots. Verb roots cannot generally be divided up into meaningful units, but in some cases, like those listed in (412)–(414), some meaning can be extracted from a portion of the root.

(412) *dih-* 'go down, descend'

dihi-   'descend from a height', e.g., an airplane
diha-   'descend', e.g., stairs
dihu-   'cause to descend'

(413) wi- 'leave, go out of'

    wiri-   'leave a land location, or go out of a building'
    wiha-   'leave in a boat'
    wihi-   'come out of a narrow opening', as in:

        gɨra-wihi-   dirt-leave
                         'defecate'

        gasiru wihi-   canoe leave
                         'leak from a boat'

        poari wihi-   hair leave
                         'hair grows and gets long'

    wiu-   'cause to leave'

(414) we- 'get wet'

    wea-   'get wet'
    webo-   'cause to get wet'
    we-yãhã   'wet-enter', as in (415)

(415) we-yãhã-biri-yẽ
      get^wet-enter-NEG-CL
      rain-coat

5.12. Independent verb roots that frequently occur in compounds

Various verb roots can stand alone but most often are compounded with other verb roots. These roots are listed in this section together with illustrations of some of the more obscure compounds.

(416) ãí- 'carry, take'

    ãĩ-waʔgã/ãĩ-gã   carry-get^up
                             'get up and carry'

    ãĩ-bũhũ   carry-cause^to^ascend
                    'carry up'

Verb Phrase

ãĩ-dihu-	carry-causeˆtoˆdescend 'carry down'
ãí-yuri-a-	carry-goˆdown-awayˆfrom 'carry down and away'
ãĩ-pi-	carry-placeˆonˆground 'carry and place on the floor/ground'
ãĩ-peo-	carry-placeˆonˆtopˆof 'carry and place on something'
ãĩ-sã-	carry-putˆinside 'carry and put inside something'
ãĩ-siu-	carry-causeˆtoˆhang 'carry and hang up'
peabẽ-ge ãĩ-tu-	fire-LOC carry-placeˆagainst 'carry and put on a fire to cook'
peabẽ-ge ãĩ-dobo-	fire-LOC carry-set 'set off a fire'
ãĩ-dũgũ-	carry-causeˆtoˆstand 'carry and stand something up'
ãĩ-ha-/ãĩ-eha-	carry-arrive 'carry and arrive'
ãĩ-pore-	carry-package 'take out something that is inside a wrapped package'

(417) bũʔrĩ- 'head down'

bũʔrĩ-bẽrẽ-ha-/ bũʔbũ-bẽre-	headˆdown-fall-TEL 'bend head down towards the ground'
bũʔrĩ-tari-	headˆdown-pass 'put one's head down and go under something'

bũʔrĩ-bia	head^down-close 'hold one's head down for a time'
bũʔrĩ-siu	head^down-hang 'hold one's head down for a time'

(418) *api-* 'place, leave something'

In verb compounds *api-* is shortened to *-pi* and has the meaning of 'place on or towards the ground', e.g., *ãĩ-pi-* 'carry and place on the floor/ground'. In the lists of §§5.10–11 are numerous examples of *-pi* co-occurring with other verb roots. (419) is an example of *api-* occurring with several verbs in a compound.

(419) wiʔi-re   duʔri-weo-pi-gã-pɨ
      house-SPC   escape-empty-place-MOVE-HSY^3ms
      He escaped, taking everything from the house, leaving it empty.

(420) *ĩʔã-* 'see' (*yã-* in the *sũbũpero porã* dialect)

ĩʔã-dihu-	see-cause^to^descend 'look down'
ĩʔã-bũhũ-	see-cause^to^ascend 'look up'
ĩʔã-bẽ-dihu-	see-force-cause^to^descend 'put one's head down to look at something'
ĩʔã-bɨrĩ-a	see-ascend-away^from 'go up to look'
ĩʔã-bũhũ-/ ĩʔa-bẽ-bũhũ-	see-cause^to^ascend/see-force-cause^to^ascend 'raise one's head to look'
ĩʔã-beo-	see-throw 'look at something a long way away'
ĩʔã-kuri-	see-travel 'visit'

Verb Phrase

ĩʔ-u-	see-do^carefully	
	'look carefully to see from a distance'	
ĩʔã-bãrĩ-	see-not^be	
	'be amazed'	
ĩʔa-yea-	see-play	
	'laugh, smile'	
ĩʔã-kũ-	see-copy	
	'copy' (-kũ is an infrequent bound verb root that has the meaning of 'imitate')	
ĩʔã-kũ-dũgũ-	see-copy-cause^to^stand	
	'look everything over, making a plan, create' as in (421)	

(421) ĩgɨ poe ii-bo-ro-re ĩʔã-kũ-dũgũ eha-pɨ
 3ms field do-POT-DVB-SPC see-copy-stand arrive-HSY^3ms
 He went and looked over and planned out the field he was going to make.

(422) -yã (from ĩʔã-) means 'try something out, prove' when it follows another root

ĩã-yã-	see-try	
	'take a look and see' (a repeat of the same root)	
keo-yã-	measure-try	
	'measure to check out'	
yoe-yã	incline^head-see	
	'take a look inside with one's head inclined'	
bãhĩ-yã-	turn-see	
	'turn and look back'	
yuʔa-yã-bũhũ-	put^head^back-see-cause^to^ascend	
	'put one's head back to take a look up'	

      ba-yã-   eat-try
                    'try out eating something' as in (423)

(423) *bãta*   *ba-yã-biri-di-rã*   *árĩ-rã*   *ii-bã*
     immediate eat-prove-NEG-PST-ANp be-ANp do-3p
     Right from the first they didn't try eating it.

(424) *pee-* 'hear, listen'

     pee-beo   hear-throw
                 'hear a report from somewhere else, hear from a distance'

     pee-kũ-   hear-copy
                 'pay careful attention to, imitate'

     pee-ãĩ-   hear-carry
                 'pay careful attention to'

     pee-yẽã-   hear-grab
                 'pay careful attention to'

     pee-u-   hear-do^carefully
                 'try to distinguish sounds from a distance, listen carefully'

     pee-bẽ-   hear-force
                 'listen hard'

     pee-aku-   hear-put^inside
                 'hear something from a distance'

(425) *were-* 'say'

     were-sã-   say-put^inside
                 'accuse'

     were-tabũ-   say-help
                 'discuss, contract'

Verb Phrase

    were-tari-   say-pass
                            'confess'

    were-sere   say-?
                            'explain'

    were-dīgī   say-CONTIN
                            'talk'

    were-yea-   say-play
                            'make fun of, tease'

(426) *-ta* 'make a cut'

    dibu-ta   cutˆwithˆscissors-cut
                     'cut cloth/paper with scissors'

    tabe-ta   chop-cut
                     'chop/cut wood with an axe or machete'

    paa-ta   hit-cut
                   'hit/cut using an axe or machete'

    kɨʔra-ta   step-cut
                     'step on something sharp and cut one's foot'

    bõʔ-ta   hand-cut
                   'tearing with hands, e.g., manioc bread, casaba'

    yã-ta   palm/hand-cut
                 'hold something in the hand, e.g., a knife, and cut'

    wíri-ta   slice-cut
                 'saw'

(427) *sī-* 'stretch out'

    sī-būhū   stretch-causeˆtoˆascend
                   'raise outstretched arm or something else'

    sī-dihu   stretch-causeˆtoˆdescend
                   'lower outstretched arm or something else'

    sĩ-beo   stretch-throw
                   'stretch straight out'

(428) *sira/siri* 'scatter'

    sira-béo   scatter-throw
                   'scatter liquid'

    ii-siri   do-scatter
                   'scatter something'

    wa-siri   go-scatter
                   'disperse'

    siri-diha   scatter-goˆdown
                   'scatter and spread throughout'

    buru-siri   comeˆapart-scatter
                   'disintegrate' as in (429)

(429) yukɨ-dɨka sora-kɨ̃ yãi-a   buru-siri-diha
     tree-fruit cook-SR getˆdone-PERF comeˆapart-scatter-descend

    waʔa-a
    go-NON3ˆPRES
When fruit is cooked, it cooks so that it comes apart and scatters (disintegrates) throughout the liquid.

The compounds in (430) also involve *sĩ-* but appear to be unrelated to the verb meaning 'stretch out'.[22]

(430) *sĩ-aĩ-*   *sĩ-* carry   'breathe'
      sĩ-yãhã- *sĩ-* enter   'relax'
      sĩ-ri   'die (not breathe)'

Examples (431)–(433) illustrate word-compounding in which the meaning changes drastically.

---

[22] The word *sĩpudiru* 'index finger' comes from *sĩ-*. The word *sĩporã* (*sĩ-* 'children') 'heart' also seems to come from *sĩ-*.

Verb Phrase

(431) *be?o-béo-* 'throw' has the meaning of 'send or do from a distance' when in a compound:

    goha-béo-   write-throw
                  'write and send a distance away'

    pee-béo-   hear-throw
                  'hear, listen from a distance, or get a message from far away'

    o-béo-   give-throw
              'send'

(432) *dɨ̃hɨ̃-* 'cry, whine' (a baby), 'chirp' (a baby bird)

    dɨ̃hɨ̃-po-   cry-mother
                 'be pregnant' (*-po* is shortened from *pago*)

    dɨ̃hɨ̃-so-   cry-rest
                'comfort (a baby)'

    dɨ̃hɨ̃-yea-   cry-foolˆaround
                 'cry and not play, act lazy, unenergetic'

See also the verbal nouns:

    dɨ̃hɨ̃-go/gɨ/rã   child-NOM
                      'child/baby, children' (some dialects only)

    dɨ̃hɨ̃-su?ri-ro   cry-nest/clothes-SING
                     'uterus'

(433) *wẽhẽ-* 'weave loosely as is done on a *puɨbu* basket'

    wẽhẽ-tu-   weave-putˆagainst
                'gesture'

    wẽhẽ-siri-   weave-scatter
               'shake one's hand or sprinkle something'

In addition, there are many more instances of verb roots compounding to form a lexical verb, or combining to expand the meaning of the verb. The example in (434) is a compound that forms the word 'slide'. It is composed of *sīgū-* 'slide along the ground', plus *-bāā-* 'unplanned/accidental', followed by *-diha* 'go straight down'. Example (435) shows a verb compound composed of a bound root plus two independent roots.

(434) bã-ge   sīgū-bāā-diha-go   igo ya-bu-re
      trail-LOC slide-accidentally-descend-fs 3fs GEN-CL-SPC

      kóã-bõ
      throw^away-3fs
      Sliding on the trail she threw away her basket.

(435) peyo-re   kɨʔra-bia-acu-pɨ
      turtle-SPC step^on-close-put^inside-HSY^3ms
      He *(danta)* stepped on the turtle burying him under the ground.

In (436), two verb roots are combined giving the idea that the first root is subject of the second.

(436) gui-sã-   fear-put^inside
             'fear for'

      dɨkɨ-diu- be^heavy-put^pressure^on
              'put pressure on with something heavy', e.g., when carrying a baby against the abdomen

5.13. Noun incorporation

Nouns are considered to be incorporated when they form one stress group with the verb and when nothing comes between the noun and the verb, e.g., the case marker *-re* would not appear on the noun. In most cases there is some change in meaning. The change in meaning and the fact that this process is no longer productive indicates that noun incorporation has been lexicalized in Desano. Examples (437)–(438) show incorporation of objects and incorporation of subjects, respectively.

(437) Incorporation of objects

      bõhõ-koe-   hand-wash
                 'wash one's hands after eating' (*bõhõ* is shortened from *bõhõtõ* 'hand')

Verb Phrase

    bõhõtõ-diri-   hand-tie
                        'marry'

    yeba-ta-   land-cut
                        'survey, make limits'

    diu-pi-   egg-place^on^ground
                        'lay an egg'

    deko-waa-   water-get
                        'get water'

(438) Incorporation of subjects

    deko-tari-   water-pass
                        'drip'

    kui-bĩũ-   eye-receive^bright^light
                        'squint because of brilliant light'

    bãsã-pore-   people-multiply
                        'procreate'

    bãsã-deyoa   people-appear
                        'be born'

    yoho-pore-   diarrhea-multiply
                        'have a bad case of diarrhea'

The following consist of a nominalized verb in compound with a verb.[23]

(439)   *iari-beha-*   desire-settle^on
                          'lust after'

       iari-bãrĩ-   desire-not^be
                          'not be desirable to the opposite sex'

---

[23] In Tucano, a closely related language, the verb 'desire' has the form *i?a-*, and occurs independently. In Desano, *ia-* does not occur by itself; rather, with the addition of the deverbalizer *-ri*, *ia-ri* has become lexicalized as a bound noun.

5.14. Denominalization

There are several derivational suffixes in Desano that are used to derive verbs from nouns. The most productive is -kɨ that makes a possessive verb out of a noun, as listed in (440) and illustrated in (441)–(442).

(440)
waha	'pay/value'	waha-kɨ-	'have value'
bārāpo	'wife'	bārāpo-kɨ-	'have a wife'
wiʔi	'house'	wiʔi-kɨ-	'have a house'
porã	'children'	porã-kɨ-	'have a child'
oko	'medicine'	oko-kɨ	'be given medicine'
wãĩ	'name'	wãĩ-kɨ	'have a name (be called)'
di	'flesh, substance'	di-kɨ	'contain, be fat'
dore	'sickness'	dore-kɨ	'be sick'
sĩporã	'heart'	sĩporã-kɨ	'have emotion'

(441) yẽ-ro   sĩporã-kɨ-bĩ
be^bad-DVB heart-VB-3ms
He is sad, angry.

(442) õã-ro   sĩporã-kɨ-a
be^good-DVB heart-VB-NON3^PRES
I am happy.

The word sĩporã 'heart' can be used in a special metaphorical sense, as in (443)–(444).

(443) sĩporã bãra-k-a   yɨ-re
heart not^be-ASSUM-NON3^PRES 1s-SPC
I was very worried.

(444) sĩporã kóã-kã-k-a
heart throw^away-ABS-ASSUM-NON3^PRES
I was startled.

-kɨ can also be added to most nominalized verbs as in (445).

(445) buʔe-ri-kɨ-bã
study-DVB-VB-3p
They have studies.

Verb Phrase

-ye added to a noun as in (446) has the meaning of 'give'. Verbs derived with -ye are bitransitive as in (447)–(448).

(446) oko   'medicine'   oko-ye-   'give medicine, treat sickness'
       waĩ   'name'   waĩ-ye-   'to name'
       waha   'pay'   waha-ye-   'to pay'
       dore   'sickness'   dore-ye-   'poison, make sick'

(447) ẽrã bāgɨ-re Guire wāĩ-ye-bã
      3p son-SPC Bill name-VB-3p
      They named their son Bill.

(448) õã-ri   oko-re   oko-ye-bã   yɨ pago-re
      be^good-DVB   medicine-SPC   medicine-VB-3p 1s mother-SPC
      They gave my mother the good medicine.

-a 'perfect' (§5.5) added to a noun gives the meaning of 'make into' as in (449).

(449) deko   'water'   deko-a   'melt'
       tore   'hole'   tore-a   'make a hole'
       bero   'circle'   be?ro-a   'make circle'

waha 'pay' combined with -ta (wahata-) gives the meaning 'earn'. There are no other known occurrences of this process.

The denominalized noun, which may already be a nominalized verb, can take a deverbalizer to become a noun again. The most common occurrence of this is shown in (450).

(450) ẽrã árĩ-ri-kɨ-ri
      3p be-DVB-VB-DVB
      their way of life

6
Valence Changing Operations

This chapter discusses valence increasing and valence decreasing operations.

6.1. Valence increasing operations

Valence increasing operations are causative, benefactive, and possessor upgrading.

Causatives. Desano has lexical, morphological and analytic causatives. The lexical causatives code highly direct causation; the morphological, less direct; and the analytic, the least direct; thus making Desano consistent with Haiman's iconicity principle that conceptual distance between cause and effect generally is reflected in formal distance between grammatical instantiation of cause and grammatical instantiation of effect (Haiman 1983:783).

Desano has just a few examples of lexical causatives because causation is so productive morphologically and analytically. Three examples are given in (451) of lexical verbs whose causative counterparts are morphologically completely distinct.

(451)
noncausative		causative	
sīrī-	'die'	*wẽhẽ-*	'kill'
ba-	'eat'	*eho-*	'feed'
i?ri-	'drink'	*tīã-*	'give to drink'

There are four MORPHOLOGICAL causatives. The first involves what appears to be a change in the verb root but is probably a lexicalized form consisting of the verb root plus a suffix. The other three are suffixes which follow the verb root.

The first MORPHOLOGICAL causative could be termed morpholexical because the change occurs within the verb root, and the type of change that occurs is not usually predictable. Generally the change involves replacing the second syllable or final vowel with bo/bõ/bū or o/u. Example (452) lists a range of functions associated with the morphological causative operators in Desano.

(452)

Root		Stem with causative	
bāhã-	'ascend'	būhū-	'raise'
bãsã-	'grow (animate)'	bãsū-	'raise (e.g., a child)'
bīrī-	'drown'	bīu-	'cause to drown'
kãrī-	'sleep'	kãbū-	'put to sleep'
wiri-	'leave'	wiu-	'cause to leave, evict'
ĩã-	'see'	ĩʔbū-	'show'
diha-	'descend'	dihu-	'lower'
tari-	'pass'	tau-	'save'
ɨka-	'be frightened'	ɨku-	'frighten'
doa-	'sit'	dobo-	'seat/set'
dedere-	'be lost'	dedeo-	'lose'
bɨhawere-	'be sad'	bɨhaweo-	'make sad'
gãbēdẽre-	'gather together'	gãbēdẽo-	'collect together'
peʔre-	'be complete'	peʔo-	'complete'
dĩgĩ-	'stand'	dūgū-	'place standing'
sia-	'hang (e.g., in a hammock)'	siu-	'cause to hang'
wãʔgã-	'get up'	wãʔgū-	'get someone up'
wea-	'get wet'	webo-	'get someone/something wet'
waʔri-	'break'	waa-	'cause to break'
yuri-	'go downriver'	yuu-	'make someone/something go downriver'
duha-	'return'	duhu-	'cause to return'
dũʔrĩ-	'break'	dũa-	'cause to break'
pãrī-	'be open'	pãgū-	'open'

Valence Changing Operations 115

The second group of morphological causatives listed in (453) differ from the first in that there is an addition rather than a change to the verb root. After the vowel *u*, the causative is *-pu*, whereas after the vowel *o*, the causative is *-po*.

(453) usi-   'be sharp'   usi-pu-   'sharpen'
      kōyō-   'be warm'   kōyō-po-   'warm up'
      sĩã-   'illuminate'   sĩã-go   'light (a lamp)'

The third morphological causative is formed by adding the verb root *dore* 'order' to another verb root, transitive or intransitive. Although *dore* is a verb root, in this construction it is phonologically attached to the preceding verb root and to the suffixes which follow; *dore-* is an example of a noncoercive causative as in (454)–(455). In (456), since one cannot order something inanimate to do something, the idea is that the person toasting the flour is causing it to get really brown. These examples indicate that the ordered event was carried out. If the order had not been carried out, the frustrative *-ri* would have been added, as in (457).

(454) ẽrã pagɨ   ẽrã-re   wa-dore-bĩ
      3p   father 3p-SPC   go-order-3ms
      Their father ordered them to go.

(455) erop-ii-gɨ   Tulio-re   iri-re   pe?o-dore-a-bɨ
      thus-do-ms   Tulio-SPC   this-SPC   finish-order-RECˆPST-NON3ˆPST
      I ordered Tulio to finish it.

(456) õã-ro   dia-ri   wa-dore-rã
      beˆgood-DVB   beˆred-DVB   go-order-ANp
      causing it to get really red (brown)

(457) igo-re   bõ?bẽ-dore-ri-bĩ
      3fs-SPC   work-order-FRUST-3ms
      He ordered her to work (but she didn't).

The fourth morphological suffix is *-tabū* which occurs following the verb root and indicates that the action is to help someone else. Although it is defined as a morphological causative, its predicate calculus would be HELP(X,P) -X helps P rather than CAUSE(X,P) -X causes P as in (458)–(460). A grammaticalized form of *-tabū* is its combination with *were-* 'say' giving the meaning 'discuss or converse' as in (461)–(462).

(458) g⫯a ērā-re dīkū sea-tabū-b⫯
 1x 3p-SPC dirt dig-help-NON3^PST
 We helped them dig dirt.

(459) Lino Ape-re   bõʔbē-tabū-g⫯ ii-bĩ   wiʔi-re
 Lino Ape-SPC work-help-ms   do-3ms house-SPC
 Lino is helping Alfred work (on) the house.

(460) g⫯a-re ii-tabū-b⫯rĩ-bĩ
 1x-SPC do-help-HAB-3ms
 He always helps us.

(461) bāsā   bērā weretabū-tuʔa-ha-b⫯
 people with discuss-COMPLET-TEL-NON3^PST
 I've already discussed it with the people.

(462) igo-re õā-ro   weretabū-biri-b⫯   doʔpa
 3fs-SPC be^good-DVB discuss-NEG-NON3^PST yet
 I haven't talked it over well with her yet.

The ANALYTIC causative 'make to do' is frequently used in Desano and can involve any verb. It consists of the verb root plus -k⫯ (switch reference) followed by the verb ii- 'do' to which are attached whatever suffixes are appropriate, including evidentials and agreement markers.[24] The causee of the verb root may be marked by -re whether the verb root is intransitive or transitive. Examples (463)–(465) show intransitive caused events and (466)–(467) show transitive caused events.

(463) õā-ro   dia-ri   deko wa-k⫯ ii-a   iri
 be^good-DVB be^red-DVB water go-SR do-NON3^PRES this
 This makes the water get really red.

(464) wātĩ ērā-re eropa wa-k⫯ ii-bĩ
 devil 3p-SPC thus go-SR do-3ms
 The devil made them do it/made that happen to them like that.

(465) ⫯i-ro   ii-k⫯ (bārĩ-re) paru   pūrĩ-k⫯ ii-a
 be^thick-DVB do-SR (1i-SPC) stomach hurt-SR do-NON3^PRES
 If you make it thick, it causes (our) stomach to hurt.

---

[24]This verb combination is an 'explicit chain'; see §10.8.

Valence Changing Operations

(466) ẽrã gɨa-re bāsĩ-biri-bu-ra-re   bāsĩ-kɨ   ii-bã
      3p   1x-SPC know-NEG-POT-DVB-SPC   know-SR   do-3p
      They taught us (lit., caused us to know) what we hadn't known (or what we would not have known).

(467) erop-ii-gɨ   ĩgɨ   bārĩ-sã-re   ĩgɨ   dore-ri-re   opa-kɨ   ii-bĩ
      thus-do-ms   3ms   1i-also-SPC   3ms   order-DVB-SPC   have-SR do-3ms
      Therefore he causes us to have his power.

Benefactive. The benefactive marker *-basa* follows the verb root and precedes the evidential marker. It indicates that the action is being done for or on behalf of someone else. An argument is added as the indirect object of *-basa*, so that the sentence may then have two indirect objects, both marked with *-re* as in (471). The benefactee may not be named but deduced from the context, as in examples (468) and (469), or marked with *-re*, which occurs on three separate items in (471).

(468) yɨ   bãrapo   árĩ-bu-ri   Gõābɨ-re   sẽrẽ-basa-ke
      1s   wife   be-POT-DVB   God-SPC   ask-BEN-IMP
      Ask God on behalf of (pray for) my wife (my wife's well-being)!

(469) yuhu   beka   do?pa   boka-basa-bo-ku-ri
      one   scholarship how   find-BEN-POT-ASSUM-Q
      How will you find a scholarship (for my brother)?

(470) pɨ?rɨ   yɨ-re   peaye-basa-bĩ   Manuel
      after   1s-SPC   shoot-BEN-3ms   Manuel
      After (killing a monkey) Manuel shot (one) for me.

(471) gahi-re   gɨa-re   Gõābɨ-re   sẽrẽ-basa-ke
      other-SPC   1x-SPC   God-SPC   ask-BEN-IMP
      Ask God about something else for us!

Possessor upgrading. In Desano various intransitive verbs in univalent propositions change to become bivalent propositions by the addition of the experiencer marked with *-re* (§4.1). Two of these valence increasing operations are possessor ascension as in (472)–(473) and accusative of interest as in (474)–(476). (Cf. also genitive constructions with *ya* (genitive) in §3.7.)

(472) igo-re   guburo bihi-ri-ru   pūrĩ-ri-ru   wiri-bɨ
      3fs-SPC   foot   swell-DVB-CL   hurt-DVB-CL   leave-NON3^PST
      (My mother's) foot was swollen and hurting (to her).

(473) bãrĩ porã   bãrĩ-re   bãsã-bea-bã
      1i   children   1i-SPC   grow-NEG-3p
      Our children don't grow (they die young).

(474) gɨa-re diasa-ro   duha-bɨ
      1x-SPC be^difficult-n   remain-NON3^PST
      It was difficult for us.

(475) õã-pũrĩ-k-a   yɨ-re
      be^good-INTEN-ASSUM-NON3^PRES   1s-SPC
      It's good to me (in my opinion).

(476) eropa wa-bɨ   ẽrã-re
      thus   go-NON3^PST   3p-SPC
      It went thusly for them.

6.2. Valence decreasing operations

Valence decreasing operations involve reflexives, reciprocals, and passive constructions.

Reflexives/reciprocals. The reflexive/reciprocal is coded analytically with the term *basi* occurring following the subject noun or pronoun. No distinct patient argument is expressed; *basi* is both reflexive (477) and reciprocal (478).

(477) tabe-bɨ   yɨ   basi
      cut-NON3^PST   1s   REFL
      I cut myself.

(478) were-tari-ro gã?bẽ-a   bãrĩ basi
      say-INTEN-n   want-NON3^PRES   1i   REFL
      We need to confess to one another.

The reflexive can also occur in a univalent clause, as in (479).

Valence Changing Operations

(479) yɨʔɨ basi ore-kere-gɨ-ta piyu-yã-bɨ
    1s REFL cry-CONCES-ms-LIM call-prove-NON3^PST
    Even though I myself was crying, I tried calling him.

A second type of reciprocal is coded by the marker *gãbẽ* which generally occurs just before the verb. It indicates that the action is done back and forth between two participants rather than by one participant. It also frequently occurs with *basi* as in (480) and (481). In (483) *gãbẽ* occurs before the adverb *õãro* 'well' in the verb phrase.

(480) gɨa basi gãbẽ weretabũ ii-bɨ
    1x REFL RECIP discuss do-NON3^PST
    We conversed among ourselves with each another.

(481) ẽrã basi gãbẽ turi-bã
    3p REFL RECIP scold-3p
    They themselves fight each other (with words).

(482) Ñu bẽrã gãbẽ kẽã-bã bãloka-ge
    John with RECIP fight-3p communal^house-LOC
    They and John fought each other in the communal house.

(483) gɨa ĩgɨ̃ bẽrã gãbẽ õã-ro ĩã-bɨ
    1x 3ms with RECIP be^good-DVB see-NON3^PST
    We got along well together.

Usually the word 'meet' occurs in a transitive clause because there is a greeter (the host) and a greeted one (the visitor). In example (484), however, with the reciprocal, all the participants equally initiate and receive the action.

(484) iri bãʔã ohogoro-ge gãbẽ bokatĩri-bɨ wapikɨ-rã-ge
    this trail end-LOC RECIP meet-NON3^PST four-ANp-LOC
    At the end of this trail we four met up with each other.

The reciprocal verb *gãbẽdẽrẽ* 'meet together' has been lexicalized as an idiom; the original meaning of *dẽrẽ* is unknown.

(485) árĩ-peʔre-rã yuhu wiʔi gãbẽ dẽrẽ-yõ-rã
    be-TOTAL-ANp one house RECIP UNKOWN-HSY-ANp
    They all gathered together in one house.

Passive constructions. Desano has an affirmative and a negative passive construction. In the affirmative construction, the passive marker is the suffix -sũ which follows the verb root and precedes the evidentials. In the negative construction, -ya follows the verb root and is then followed by the verb bãrĩ- 'not be', followed by the evidential. In clauses marked with the passive suffixes, the agent is either not expressed or may be marked with -re; the patient is promoted to subject of the clause with resulting verb agreement, but sometimes it is still marked with -re. Examples (486)–(487) are taken from a text concerning which animals are eaten and which are not.

(486) õã   yãbã-re   ba-sũ-ko-bã   wekɨ-a yese-a
     these deer-SPC   eat-PASS-ASSUM-3p   cow-p pig-p

     ba-sũ-ko-bã
     eat-PASS-ASSUM-3p
     Deer are eaten; cows, and pigs are eaten.

(487) pĩrũ-a-sã   ba-ya   bãrĩ-bã   ẽrã ta-bẽrã
     snake-p-also eat-PASS not^be-3p   3p   LIM-with
     Snakes also are not eaten.

(488) i   wiʔi   dẽ   pãgũ-ya   bãrĩ-yo-ro
     this house first   cause^to^open-PASS   not^be-HSY-NON3
     This house wasn't opened.

(489) bãrĩ yẽ-ri-re   duʔu-ya   bãri-a
     1i   be^bad-DVB-SPC   leave^off-PASS not^be-NON3^PRES
     The bad is not left off (we don't stop doing bad things).

Example (490) illustrates a special negative form with the verb 'be able' plus the negative passive construction. Verb agreement is in the neuter gender (NON3). The construction conveys the meaning of 'it is impossible'.

(490) deko-dɨ   kuri-bã   bãsĩ-ya   bãrĩ-roka
     water-day   travel-POT   be^able-PASS   not^be-PROB^NON3
     On a rainy day it is impossible to travel.

The passive marker -sũ also occurs with the deontic construction (§5.4) as in examples (491)–(492).

Valence Changing Operations

(491) *Gõãbɨ gãbē-biri-kɨ-ta   baye-kere-ta   bārī sīrī-a*
God   want-NEG-SR-LIM chant-CONCES-LIM 1i die-PERF

wa-sū-ro   gã?bē-a
go-PASS-DVB want-NON3^PRES

If God doesn't want it, even though chanting is done we have to die (it happens that we die).

(492) *pasiri-pe?o īā-bē-būhū-gɨ   kuiri yāhā-sū-ro*
chop-TOTAL see-force-cause^to^ascend-ms eyes enter-PASS-n

gã?bē-a   ērā-gā-sā-re
want-NON3^PRES 3p-DIM-also-SPC

If you look up while cutting down (a tree), these tiny (ants) (happen to) enter in your eyes (lit., your eyes happen to be entered by these tiny ones).

There are a few verbs that are lexically passive. Two examples are *pabu-* 'be hit or shot (with a gun)' in (493) and *kõ?bõ-* 'be bitten (by a snake, animal, scorpion)' in (494); *pabu-* seems to be the causative form of *pa-* 'hit', and *kõ?bo-* seems to be the causative form of *kūrī-* 'bite'.

(493) *īgɨ pabu-a   wa-gɨ kari-bī*
3ms be^hit-PERF go-ms seem-ms
It seems he has been hit.

(494) *āyā-re kõ?bõ-di-rā   árī-bā*
snake-SPC be^bitten-PST-ANp be-3p
They were bitten by a snake.

The passive markers are also used like a 'middle', when there is no suggestion that an agent caused the event to happen to the patient (the subject); (495) is an example of a middle with *-sū*.

(495) *īgɨ apīritodiuri bihi-sū-bī*
ms   testicles   swell-PASS-3ms
His testicles are swollen.

The passive suffix *-ya* is also used as a suffix of middle voice when it is added to transitive roots, producing stative verbs listed in (496). Unlike Siona, Desano does not have examples of the same verbs in three voices, middle, active, and causative.

(496) peo-   'set on'   peya-   'be perched'
     tu-   'put up against'   tu?ya- 'be up against'
     dɨ?a- 'save'   dɨ?ya- 'be leftover, lack'
     sua-   'weave'   suya-   'be situated between two things'
     do?o- 'connect'   do?ya- 'be connected'
     yaa-   'bury'   yaya-   'be buried'

7

Sentence Structure

Sentences consist of one or more clauses, with one clause obligatorily an independent clause, which usually occurs sentence final. Nonfinal, subordinate clauses may be marked for temporal or logical arguments or may be unmarked. For a description of nonfinal clauses, see chapter 10. The sentence frequently begins with a connecting phrase or clause (see chapter 11 for a discussion of connectors between sentences). Included in the sentence are noun phrases which function as subjects, objects, and obliques. Although the basic constituent order in the sentence is SOV (§1.1), with oblique also preceding the verb and nonfinal clauses preceding the final clause, there is great variation in order of constituents (see §11.5 for some pragmatic factors affecting constituent order).

This chapter discusses the basic sentence types of intransitive, transitive, and bitransitive (also called ditransitive), and demonstrates that Desano has a nominative/accusative system for coding grammatical relations. Also discussed in this chapter are predicate nominals and adjectives, existential and predicate locative constructions, and possessive constructions.

7.1. Intransitive, transitive, and bitransitive clauses

Desano has simple univalent (intransitive), bivalent (transitive), and trivalent (bitransitive) clauses.

UNIVALENT clauses consist minimally of an obligatory intransitive verb as in (496)–(497).

(497) *wa-dia-bea-bĩ*
go-DESID-NEG-3ms
He does not want to go.

(498) *professor-sã   era-biri-bĩ   do?pa*
professor-also arrive-NEG-3ms yet
The professor also hadn't arrived yet.

BIVALENT clauses consist of an obligatory transitive verb and a direct object, which may or may not be marked with the case marker *-re* (§4.1). The subject does not have to be expressed when it is known from the context.

(499) *oho   ote-a*
banana plant-NON3ˆPRES
We plant banana.

(500) *gɨa-re dẽ   yuhu-gɨ dore-biri-bĩ*
1x-SPC first one-ms order-NEG-3ms
No one ordered us (to come).

(501) *Jairo gɨa-re sẽrẽpi-bĩ daha*
Harry 1x-SPC ask-3ms again
Harry asked us again/next.

(502) *tu?a-ha   yɨ-re   kóã-dia-bĩ*
finish-TEL 1s-SPC throwˆout-DESID-3ms
After that, he wanted to expel me (from school).

TRIVALENT clauses consist of an obligatory bitransitive verb with a direct and an indirect object. The indirect object is always marked with *-re* (specifier). The direct object may or may not be marked. The subject is indicated by verb agreement and may or may not be named; see examples (503)–(504). In discourse, all three arguments seldom appear in the trivalent clause.

(503) *gɨa-re biasoro   dobo ii-bã*
1x-SPC pepperˆpot set   do-3p
They gave us a hot pepper dish.

(504) *ẽrã   õã-dore-beo-ra-re   gɨa-re were ii-bĩ*
3p   beˆgood-order-send-DVB-SPC 1x-SPC say   do-3ms
He gave us the greetings that they sent.

The examples in this section illustrate the grouping of subject and agent as against patient to give proof of Desano displaying a

Sentence Structure 125

nominative/accusative system of coding grammatical relations. The subject of a univalent clause (S), and the agent of a bivalent clause (A) are coded on the verb with the same suffixes. Examples (498), (500), and (501) show that the verb agrees with S and with A. In example (498), the suffix -bĩ refers to the singular masculine S argument. In examples (500) and (501), the same suffix agrees with the third masculine A arguments 'not one' and 'Harry', respectively. When the patient of a bivalent clause (P) is definite, it is distinguished by the case marker -re which occurs as a suffix on nouns, pronouns, and nominalized clauses.

7.2. Predicate nominals and predicate adjectives

Predicate nominals consist minimally of a predicate noun phrase followed by an affirmative or negative form of the verb árĩ/ã?rĩ- 'be'. If the subject noun phrase is expressed, it typically precedes the predicate. There are virtually no predicate adjectives in Desano, as adjectival concepts are normally expressed by nominalizing a stative verb (see §3.8). Examples of the affirmative predicate nominal construction are given in (505)–(507).

(505) bɨʔɨ pago   gaki   ã?rĩ-bõ
      2s   mother monkey   be-3fs
      Your mother is a monkey.

(506) wɨa-gɨ   ã?rĩ-bĩ
      beˆlarge-ms   be-3ms
      He (tick) is large (lit., a large one).

(507) bɨ-ya-ru   gasiru bābā-ru āhrã-a
      2s-GEN-CL canoe   new-CL   be-NON3ˆPRES
      Your boat is a new one.

Example (508) shows the negative predicate nominal construction; and in (509), the negative particle bēhē plus the limiter -ta (§9.3) are used to negativize a predicate nominal.

(508) ũʔrã   árĩ-bea-a
      howlerˆmonkey   be-NEG-NON3ˆPRES
      (You) aren't a howler monkey.

(509) ĩgɨ̃ yẽ-gɨ   bẽhẽ-ta   ã?rĩ-bĩ
      3ms be^bad-ms NEG-LIM   be-3ms
      He is not bad (a bad person).

In example (510), the subject, expressed by two noun phrases, is distinguished by being marked with the focus of contrast marker -pɨ, which would not occur on the predicate (§11.1).

(510) yuhu-gɨ peabãsɨ̃-pɨ   Ever wãĩ-kɨ-gɨ-pɨ   taboa   wiri-gɨ
      one-ms   white^man-FOC   Ever name-VB-ms-FOC   boards saw-ms

      árĩ-bĩ
      be-3ms
      A white man (non-Indian) named Ever was a carpenter.

An adverbial phrase can be the predicate, as in (511), in which it occurs before the subject.

(511) gahi-ro-pa   ẽrã-sã   ã?rĩ-bã
      other-n-MAN   3p-also   be-3p
      They also are different.

7.3. Existential and predicate locative constructions

There is no syntactic difference in Desano between existential and predicate locative constructions. Furthermore, they have the same basic structure as the predicate nominals (§7.2). These constructions are formed with the verb árĩ- 'be' for positive constructions and bãrĩ- 'not be' for the negative, with an optional locative/time phrase marked, when appropriate, with the locative marker -ge and/or the case-marker -re (see §4.1–2). Examples (512)–(514) illustrate the positive construction.

(512) tẽhẽ-a   árĩ-yũ-bã
      tick-p   be-ASSUM-3p
      There were ticks (lit., ticks were).

(513) õã   boso-a-re   árĩ-yũ-bã   tẽhẽ-a
      these   boso-p-SPC   be-ASSUM-3p   tick-p
      There were ticks on the *boso* (rodent).

(514) oho-sã   baha   árĩ-k-a
      banana-also a^lot   be-ASSUM-NON3^PRES
      There are also many kinds of bananas.

For the Desanos, the statement in (515) can have two interpretations. One is that 'my mother' is not in that location; the other, that she is dead (doesn't exist).

(515) yɨ pago   bãrĩ-bõ
      1s mother not^be-3fs
      My mother isn't.

The example in (516) illustrates a predicate locative with a locative and a time phrase.

(516) yɨʔɨ peʔyarã   poʔro-ge 6 abe-ri   árĩ-bɨ
      1s   brothers^in^law near-LOC 6 month-p be-NON3^PST
      I was at my brothers-in-law's for six months.

7.4. Possessive constructions

There are various ways to indicate possession or lack of possession in Desano. One is by use of the verbalizer -kɨ on a noun which indicates a permanent state rather than a temporary possession, as in (517). Another way is by use of the verb opa- 'have' which indicates positive possession, or by the negative of this verb bõo- 'not have'; the sentences in (518), taken from one text, illustrate the use of opa- and bõo-.

(517) bãrapo-kɨ-bĩ
      wife-VB-3ms
      He has a wife.

(518) bãrĩ dipari bãhã-rã poe-ri bõo-rã dẽ bari
　　　 1i　 indian　PERT-ANp field-p not^have-ANp first food

　　　 bõo-a　　　　　　 dẽ ãruyẽ　　　　 dẽ yõkã
　　　 not^have-NON3^PRES first manioc^bread first manioc^drink

　　　 dẽ　 bãrĩ bõo-a　　　　　　 poe-ri opa-rã　 bãrĩ
　　　 first 1i　 not^have-NON3^PRES field-p have-ANp 1i

　　　 opa-pe?o-k-a
　　　 have-TOTAL-ASSUM-NON3^PRES
　　　 If we Indian people don't have fields, we don't have any food. We don't have any manioc bread or drink. If we have fields, we have everything.

Another way to show possession is by using the verb *árĩ-* 'be' or the verb *bãrĩ-* 'not be' with the possessor or nonpossessor marked with the object marker *-re*, and the possessed item acting as the subject of the sentence with verb agreement (see §6.1). This is illustrated from a text on ticks in (519)–(520).

(519) õã　 boso-a-re　 árĩ-yũ-bã　 tẽhẽ-a
　　　 these boso-p-SPC be-ASSUM-3p tick-p
　　　 The *boso* (rodent) has ticks/There are ticks on the *boso*.

(520) õã　 yee-a-re　 õã　 tẽhẽ-a bãri-yũ-bã
　　　 these tiger-p-SPC these tick-p not^be-ASSUM-3p
　　　 Tigers don't have ticks/There aren't ticks on tigers.

8
Question Formation

Desano questions are divided into three types: polar questions, information questions, and questions formed with particles. The first two types of questions end with the interrogative marker -*ri*, which occurs after the evidential and replaces the subject agreement markers. No distinction is made between the assumed past tense and the hearsay evidentials with the question marker; cf. (521)–(522). See (303) for an example of a question formed with the permission imperative suffix -*si*. See (360) for an example of a question formed with the dubitative suffix -*sa*.

(521) *igo segundo curso   ii-bãsĩ-ku-ri*
      3fs second   course do-ABIL-ASSUM-Q
      Can/May she do the second course?

(522) *wɨ-ri-ru   ari-tuʔa-yu-ri*
      fly-DVB-CL   come-COMPLET-HSY-Q
      Has the plane left on its way here?

8.1. Polar questions

Four functions of polar questions have been identified. They are (1) to solicit information, (2) to request action, (3) to greet, and (4) to code a purpose clause.

The most basic use of the polar question is to request information as in (523).

(523) bɨ̃ pago   poe-ge   wa?á-**ri**
    2s mother field-LOC go-Q
    Did your mother go to the field?

At times the question form is used to politely indicate to the hearer that some action is requested. It is used with the negative and usually with the potential and assumed evidential markers as in (524)–(525).

(524) ĩgɨ̃-re   bɨ̃ã ii-tabũ-biri-bo-ku-**ri**   ãrĩ-gɨ bɨ̃ã-re
    3ms-SPC 2p   do-BEN-NEG-POT-ASSUM-Q say-ms 2p-SPC

    were-a
    say-NON3^PRES
I am letting you know about this in case you want to help him. (lit., I advise you saying, "Won't you probably help him?")

(525) bɨ̃ã do?pagá bõ?bẽ-dia-biri-bo-ku-**ri**
    2p   today   work-DESID-NEG-POT-ASSUM-Q
    Would you want to work today?

The function of greeting is carried out by one or a series of questions and answers. For example, in the morning the initiator asks if the other person got up, and he replies that he did, as in example (526).

(526) wã?gã-**ri** bɨ̃   wã?gã-bɨ
    get^up-Q 2s   get^up-NON3^PST
    Did you get up?   I got up

The purpose clause is a verb plus the interrogative marker -ri, usually followed by ãrĩ- 'say', in an explicit medial clause that agrees with the main verb.

(527) erop-ii-rã   yɨ-re   eropa yɨ?ri-dĩgɨ-kã-ke   bɨ̃ã
    thus-do-ANp   1s-SPC thus   answer-CONTIN-ABS-IMP 2p

    wahata-bo-ro-re   dedeo-**ri** ãrĩ-rã
    get^pay-POT-DVB-SPC lose-Q   say-ANp
Therefore, continually keep on obeying me like that in order that you don't lose your reward (lit. saying, 'Will we lose the reward we are to get?')!

8.2. Information questions

Information questions are formed by using the interrogative pronouns which are displayed in (120). The interrogative pronouns either begin the sentence or directly follow the topic. They precede the noun they are modifying and usually take the appropriate classifier or postposition. When their role is patient, *-re* is affixed. Note the use of interrogative pronouns in (528)–(535). In (535) the interrogative pronoun *doʔpa ii-* contracts to *doʔpii-*.

(528) yuhu-ru herĩga **dipẽ** waha-kɨ-ri ero-ge-re
one-CL syringe how^much pay-VB-Q there-LOC-SPC
How much does a syringe cost there?

(529) **dõã**-re ĩa-yu-ri
who-SPC see-HSY-Q
Whom did they see?

(530) **doʔpa** ii bõʔbẽ-gɨku-ri
how do work-PROB^3ms-Q
What will I do for work?

(531) **dõʔõ**-ge vacación wa-rãku-ri gɨa
where-LOC vacation go-PROB^ANp-Q 1x
Where will we go during vacation?

(532) **doʔpa** pepi-ri bɨã
how think-Q 2p
What do you think?

(533) **doʔpa** árɨ-kɨ bãrɨ akawererã goʔra-re opɨ
what be-SR 1i relatives exactly-SPC king

aku-gɨku-ri bɨʔɨ
put^in-PROB^3ms-Q 2s
When are you going to put in one of our own relatives as king?

(534) **di-ru** gasiru bɨ-ya-ru ãʔrɨ-ri
which-CL canoe 1s-GEN-CL be-Q
Which boat is yours?

(535) **doʔpii**-rã   wa-bea-**ri** bɨã
how^do-ANp go-NEG-Q 2p
Why don't you go?

Five functions of information questions in Desano have been identified. They are (1) to solicit more elaborate information than would be available from an affirmation or disaffirmation, as in examples (528)–(535) above; (2) as a scolding device; (3) to ask a question when the speaker doesn't know the answer; (4) as an indirect question; and (5) to emphasize the extent of a question. These are elaborated and illustrated in the following discussion.

The interrogative pronoun 'why' with the question marker on the verb functions as a scolding device as in (536).

(536) **doʔpii**-gɨ   bɨ pagɨ bãgɨ-re   paa-**ri**
how^do-ms 2s father son-SPC hit-Q
Why did you hit your younger brother?

The interrogative pronoun plus verb root plus the assumed evidential in the present tense and verb agreement act as a question when the speaker doesn't know the answer as in (537).

(537) ũba   **doʔpa** ii-ku-bɨ̃
doubt how   do-ASSUM-3ms
What is he doing?

An indirect question is formed when an interrogative pronoun occurs with a nominalized subordinate clause, as in (538), or in a sentence where the interrogative pronoun and the verb with the question marker occur in the context of a main nonquestion verb, as in (539). These are actually examples of complement-taking verbs allowing, in addition to indicative complements, WH-question complements (Givón 1990:804–805) (see §10.1). In (538), there is no question marker on the verb in the subordinate clause; the interrogative pronoun occurs before the verb which is a nominalized verb followed by -re.

(538) kãrẽyã ẽrã **doʔpa** árĩ-ri-kɨ-ri-re   buʔe-bɨ
chicken 3p how   be-DVB-VB-DVB-SPC study-NON3^PST
We studied how chickens act.

Question Formation

(539) sĩʔã-ri-dɨka berã sĩʔã-yã-bɨ   **di**[25]   õã-ri
     light-DVB-CL with light-prove-NON3^PST which be^good-DVB

     diu-ri ã?rĩ-ri **di**-diu-ri-pɨ   yẽ-ri   diu-ri ã?rĩ-**ri**
     egg-p be-Q which-egg-p-FOC be^bad-DVB egg-p be-Q

     ãrĩ bãsĩ-bo-rã
     say know-POT-ANp
We shone a flashlight on the eggs to be able to know which were the good eggs and which were the bad ones.

The interrogative pronoun also functions as a quantifier or indefinite relative pronoun in a sentence to emphasize the extent of an action. In these cases the verb does not carry the interrogative *-ri* as shown in (540)–(541).

(540) **dõã** **dɨkɨ** bãrĩ-re tua-yu-bã
     who each 1i-SPC adhere-ASSUM-3p
     Many (ticks) stuck to us!

(541) **dõʔõ** bari **dõʔõ** dɨgɨ wa-rã diye-a
     where food where jungle go-ANp put^in-NON3^PRES
     Whatever food (we find) wherever we go in the jungle, we put in (the basket).

8.3. Question particles

ka has been described in section §1.10 as a question particle that occurs word final on a noun or pronoun that occurs alone in an utterance, as in (542).

(542) bɨ̃ bãgɨ **ka**
     2s son Q
     What about your son?

---

[25] In (539) *diu* is the classifier that goes with the interrogative pronoun *di*. I do not know why the *di* is not followed by *diu-ri* in the first clause of this example.

9

Negation

The standard means of forming a negative clause in Desano is by a suffix on the verb. There are also the lexically negative verbs *bārī-* 'not be' (§7.3) and *bõo-* 'not have' (§7.4), and constituent negation in the form of the negative particle *bēhē-ta* (§7.2). Negative future forms are discussed in §5.3. Negative imperatives are discussed in §5.4.

9.1. Standard clausal negation

Standard negation in Desano is accomplished in the verb by the suffix *-biri* which occurs after the verb root and before the evidentials. Modal and other suffixes may occur before or after the negative in the verb phrase. With the recent past marker *-a*, *-biri + -a* becomes *-bira*.

(543) ẽrã were-kɨ̃   pee-dia-**biri**-yũ-bã
      3p speak-SR hear-DESID-NEG-ASSUM-3p
      When they spoke, they didn't want to listen to them.

(544) õã-ro   bāsī-**bira**-bã
      beˆgood-DVB know-NEGˆRECˆPST-3p
      They didn't know well.

The negative suffix occurs on subordinated and nominalized verbs as well as on the main verb. In nominalized animate clauses in the present tense, the *-ri* of *-biri* is dropped giving *-bi*, as in (546)–(547)

(545) ẽrã were-yũ-bã   pare   Gõābɨ̃ ũbũpeo-**biri**-di-rã-re
      3p speak-ASSUM-3p finally God   believe-NEG-PST-ANp-SPC
      They spoke finally to those that didn't believe in God.

(546) gahi-rã   pee-bãsĩ-**bi**-rã   árĩ-yõ-rã
    other-ANp hear-ABIL-NEG-ANp be-HSY-ANp
    Other ones were senseless ones (lit., who were unable to listen).

(547) baha-**bi**-rã   wẽhẽ-bɨ
    a^lot-NEG-ANp kill-NON3^PST
    (I) killed not many fish (lit., fish that were not many).

(548) ẽrã gãbẽ-**biri**-ra-re   were-bã gɨa-re
    3p   want-NEG-DVB-SPC   speak-3p 1x-SPC
    They told us what they did not want.

-*biri* becomes -*bea* preceding present tense, visual evidentials.

(549) dẽ   yɨ?ri-**bea**-a   ĩgɨ   baye-ri
    first answer-NEG-NON3^PRES 3ms chant-DVB
    (The sickness) doesn't respond to his chanting (not from the beginning).

(550) bãrĩ sẽrẽ-**biri**-kɨ   ii-tabũ-**bea**-bĩ
    1i   ask-NEG-SR   do-BEN-NEG-3ms
    If we don't ask, he doesn't help.

There is a future negative suffix -*sõbẽ* 'will not do' (see §5.3) as in (551).

(551) gahi   boho-ri   buhe-**sõbẽ**
    other dry-DVB study-NEG^FUT
    Another year (I) will not study.

9.2. Lexical negation

In the transitive verb *bõo-* 'not have' and the stative verb *bãrĩ-* 'not be', the concept of negation is part and parcel of their lexical semantics as in (552) and (553) respectively. (See §7.3 for *bãrĩ-* in existential constructions and §7.4 for *bãrĩ-* and *bõo-* in possessor constructions.)

(552) bõã bõo-bã
    salt not^have-3p
    They don't have any salt.

(553) a?i-sā   bārī-di-rā   árī-bā gia eha-ki
      dad-also notˆbe-PST-ANp be-3p   1x   arrive-SR
      Dad and Mom were not there when we arrived (inferred).

9.3. Constituent negation

The negative postposition *bēhē* plus the limiter *-ta* follows nouns, pronouns, postpositional phrases, adjectives, adverbs, and subordinate clauses. It negativizes the constituent that it follows, while the verb stays in the affirmative. Like other postpositions, the specific object marker *-re* attaches to *bēhē-ta* rather than to the items that it modifies.

(554) ērā biriga go?ra   **bēhē-ta** pūri-bā
      3p   much   exactly NEG-LIM   hurt-3p
      They (certain scorpions) don't hurt much (lit., their hurting is not much).

(555) ero-re   yoa-ri   bohe bēhē-ta bõ?bē-bi
      there-SPC   long-DVB time NEG-LIM work-NON3ˆPST
      I didn't work there for very long (lit., I worked for not a long time).

(556) yi   bēhē-ta-re   paa-bĩ
      1s   NEG-LIM-SPC hit-3ms
      He didn't hit me (it wasn't me he hit).

Example (557) has a grammaticalized form with *bēhē-ta* that means 'but'. Literally the meaning would be 'about not to do' (see §11.8).

(557) ii-bu   bēhē-ta gia ari-ri   subu-ge-re   īgi
      do-POT NEG-LIM 1x   come-DVB time-LOC-SPC 3ms

      era-bira-bĩ   ero   Taraboagoro-re
      arrive-NEGˆRECˆPST-3ms   there Taraboagoro-SPC
      But, when it was time to come, he hadn't arrived there at Taraboagoro (name of their location).

9.4 Quantifier negation

The quantifier *baha* 'a lot' is negativized with the negative marker *-bi*, which becomes *-bē* preceding nasal suffixes. For example, *baha-rā* 'aˆlot-animate' becomes *baha-bē-rã* 'few-animate', and *baha* 'many inanimate' becomes *baha-bē-gã* (many-NEG-DIM) 'few inanimate'.

Otherwise, as in Barasano (Jones and Jones 1991:130), inherently negative quantifiers do not exist. They are coded either by the positive quantifier occurring with the negative verbs *bāri-* or *bōo-* as in (558), or with the constituent negative *bēhē-ta* following the quantifier as in (559).

(558) *dē   yuhu-gɨ   yɨ-re   wapikɨ-gɨ   bāri-bĩ*
      first one-ms   1s-SPC   accompany-ms   notˆbe-3ms
      There was no one to help me (lit. the one to help me wasn't).

(559) *wɨa-ro   bēhē-ta   opa-bĩ*
      much-DVB   NEG-LIM   have-3ms
      He had a little (didn't have much).

10
Subordination

Subordination in Desano includes nominalizations, which function in complementation and as constituents in noun phrases; adverbial clauses; and chained clauses (often involving switch reference markers). Adverbial clauses also involve nominalization, but are considered separately because they carry additional morphology.

10.1–10.3 Nominalizations

This section discusses markers that deverbalize a verb, types of nominalizations, and their functions.

10.1. Markers that deverbalize a verb

The suffixes listed in (560) are used to nominalize a verb. For identification, the animate suffixes are marked with their respective number and gender, and the inanimate suffixes with DVB (deverbalizer). Desano differs from Barasano in that there is no difference between those suffixes which occur when the nominalization is subject of the verb and those which occur when the nominalization is anything other than the subject (Jones and Jones 1991:142).

(560) Deverbalizing suffixes

	animate	inanimate	time/place/concept
ms	-gɨ		
fs	-go	-ri[26]	-ro
p	-rã		

If the nominalized form refers to an event that will take place in the future, the potential suffix -bu/bo precedes the deverbalizing suffix. If it refers to a past event, the suffix -di (past) precedes the deverbalizer for animate and place/time, and the deverbalizer -ri becomes -ra (-ri +-a). The table in (561) shows the possible combinations of these suffixes.

(561) Tense plus deverbalizing suffixes

			animate	inanimate concrete/ abstract noun	time/place/ concept
present	ms		-gɨ		
	fs		-go	-ri	-ro
	p		-rã		
past	ms		-di-gɨ		
	fs		-di-go	-ra	-di-ro
	p		-di-rã		
future	ms		-bu-gɨ		
	fs		-bu-go	-bu-ri	-bu-ro
	p		-bõ-rã		

In the most prestigious dialect *(boreka porã)*, -gɨ and -go are dropped and the masculine becomes -bu and the feminine -bo as in (562) and (563) respectively. -bu varies with -bo and becomes nasalized from the left (see §1.13, §1.16).

(562) wa-bu ii-bĩ
go-POT do-3ms
He is about to go.

---

[26] In the *boreka porã* dialect, -ri becomes -di before some of the classifiers, e.g., *tūrū-di-ru* (turn-DVB-CL) 'car'. To avoid confusion, the suffix is shown as -ri in all examples.

(563) kā̃rī-bo   ã?rī-bõ
sleep-POT be-fs
She is ready for sleep.

In addition to tense suffixes, suffixes of mode, aspect, direction, and negation can occur between the verb root and the deverbalizing suffix; there is no verb agreement marker. The nominalized form agrees in gender and number with its referent. Note examples (564)–(571).

(564) wai ba-gɨ   ã?rī-bī
fish eat-ms be-3ms
He is one who eats fish, i.e., a fish eater.

(565) wekɨ-re   ba-di-gɨ   era-bī
danta-SPC eat-PST-ms arrive-3ms
The one who ate the *danta* arrived.

(566) ba-ri   ã?rã-a
eat-DVB be-NON3^PRES
There is food (lit., something for eating).

(567) õ?õ   ẽrã wai ba-bɨrī-di-ro   ã?rã-a
here 3p fish eat-HAB-PST-DVB be-NON3^PRES
This is where they always ate fish.

(568) yẽ?ẽ-dõhõ-re opa-ri   bārī ba-bu-ri-re
what-CL-SPC have-Q 1i   eat-POT-DVB-SPC
What do (you) have for us to eat?

(569) ẽrã kā̃rī-bo-ro
3p sleep-POT-DVB
place where they will sleep

(570) i   yɨ?ɨ bu?e-ra   ã?rã-a
this 1s study-DVB be-NON3^PRES
This is what I studied.

(571) bu?e-dia-biri-di-rã
study-DESID-NEG-PST-ANp
the ones who didn't want to study

10.2. Types of nominalizations

Four types of nominalization are distinguished: (1) those involving animate participants, (2) inanimate action nominalizations, (3) inanimate patient and instruments, and (4) locations and time.

Nominalizations involving animate participants. Agent, subject, and animate patient nominalizations all involve the animate deverbalizers given in the tables in (560)–(561). There can be ambiguity between agent and animate patient nominalizations. For example, teacher and student are the same word as in (572).

(572) *buʔe-gɨ*
study-ms
the one who teaches or the one who studies (i.e., is taught)

Similarly, there is ambiguity in the past tense, as in (573), but the addition of the passive marker *-sũ* disambiguates the construction as in (574).

(573) *kóã-di-gɨ*
throwˆaway-PST-ms
the one who threw out or the one who was thrown out

(574) *kóã-sũ-di-gɨ*
throwˆaway-PASS-PST-ms
the one who was thrown out

Inanimate action nominalizations. Action nominalizations are obtained with the deverbalizing suffix *-ri* or its past form *-ra*; less productively, *-ro* can also form an action nominalization. Action nominalizations almost always occur with one or more arguments, and generally function as object in the matrix clause, but can also be the subject. Examples (573) and (574) show the action nominalization being used to form either a subject complement or subject of an existential construction (see §7.3). In all these roles these nominalizations can be suffixed by the appropriate case markers, as in (576).

(575) *ēhõ baye-ri   áʔrã-a*
flu chant-DVB be-NON3ˆPRES
There is chanting for the flu (lit., flu chanting).

(576) ẽrã-re gui-ri   bãrĩ-y-a   pare
      3p-SPC fear-DVB not^be-ASSUM-NON3^PRES finally
      There was no fear in them finally.

Examples (577)–(579) illustrate action nominalizations functioning as object; (578) and (579) illustrate the difference between the nominalized forms with -ri and with -ro, where -ro refers to more generalized topics and -ri to details.

(577) igo sẽrẽpi-kɨ were-bɨ   gɨa-re eropa wa-ra-re
      3fs ask-SR say-NON3^PST 1x-SPC thus go-DVB-SPC
      When she asked, I told what had happened to us.

(578) kãrẽyã ẽrã dore   opa-ri-re   ẽrã ĩgĩ wirita-ri-re
      chicken 3p sickness have-DVB-SPC 3p beak cut-DVB-SPC

      ẽrã-re eho-ri-re   baha bu?e-bɨ
      3p-SPC feed-DVB-SPC a^lot study-NON3^PST
      We studied a lot of things: the sicknesses chickens have, cutting their beaks, and feeding them.

(579) ẽrã yese-a taribu-re koe-ro   ẽrã ba-ri-re   sã-ro
      3p pig-p room-SPC wash-DVB 3p eat-DVB-SPC put^in-DVB

      bu?e-bɨ
      study-NON3^PST
      We studied washing the pig pens and putting in their food.

Inanimate patient and instrument nominalizations. For patient and instrument nominalizations, the nominalizing suffix precedes the appropriate classifiers. For nominalized verbs in the present, -ri precedes the classifier. For past nominalizations some classifiers take -di and some take -ra. Some examples of patient nominalizations are given in (580)–(583).

(580) puibu kóã-di-bu
      basket throw^away-PST-CL
      the thrown-away basket, the basket that is thrown away

(581) yɨ-re   su?ri   āsū-basa-ra-yẽ   sãyã-bɨ
      1s-SPC clothes buy-BEN-DVB-CL   put^on-NON3^PST
      I put on the dress (cloth) that was bought for me.

(582) gasiru kóã-bu-ri-ru
      canoe   throw^away-POT-DVB-CL
      the canoe that is to be thrown away

(583) oho-yũ   sĩrĩ-ri-yũ
      banana-CL   die-DVB-CL
      the dying banana plant, the banana plant that is dying

Because of the classifiers and deverbalizers in the language, Desano can productively form new instrument nominalizations, for example (584).

(584) wɨ-ri-ru
      fly-DVB-CL
      airplane (instrument for flying)

Location and time nominalizations. Location and time nominalizations are formed with the use of the deverbalizer *-ro* as in (585)–(586).

(585) gɨa bõ?bẽ-di-ro-ge
      1x   work-PST-DVB-LOC
      where we worked

(586) boyo-ro
      be^light-DVB
      at dawn

10.3. Functions of nominalizations

Two functions of nominalizations have been distinguished, i.e., nominal constituents in clauses (complementation) and constituents in noun phrases.

Nominalized forms functioning as nominal constituents in clauses (complementation). Most clauses functioning as the complement of other clauses are nominalized and may be viewed as headless

Subordination

relative clauses. Object complementation may occur with cognition verbs, utterance verbs, and manipulation verbs; and subject complementation involves actions. These are discussed and illustrated in turn.

The cognition verbs *bāsī-* 'know', *buʔe-* 'study', *īʔā-* 'see', and *pee-* 'hear' take a complement as object. They are not quite merged complements because they often code their own arguments.

(587) *kāreyā   ērā   doʔpa árī-ri-kɨ-ri-re,   ērā dore   opa-ri-re*
 chicken   3p   how   be-DVB-VB-DVB-SPC 3p sickness have-DVB-SPC

  ērā kāreyā   īgī   wirita-ri-re   baha buʔe-bɨ
  3p chicken beak cut-DVB-SPC aˆlot study-NON3ˆPST
 We studied much: how chickens are (characteristics), the sicknesses they have, cutting the chickens' beaks.

(588) *sirura-ri ea-ri-re,   kābīsa-ri ea-ri-re   bāsī-bā*
 pant-p   sew-DVB-SPC   shirt-p   sew-DVB-SPC know-3p
 They also learned (knew) how to sew pants and shirts.

(589) *bɨ̄ā bābā-rā   pee-bāsī-ke   bɨā-re pɨʔrɨ-ge   wa-bu-ri-re*
 2p new-ANp hear-know-IMP 2p-SPC after-LOC go-POT-DVB-SPC
 You young people, think and know what is going to happen to you later!

The deverbalized complement of the verbs *pee-* 'hear' and *īʔā-* 'see', however, is most often an explicit chain medial base with the switch referent marker *-kɨ* (§10.8). Such clauses frequently function as a link in narrative discourse as in (590)–(591); *pee-* 'hear' can also occur with a regular nominalized clause as in (592); and in (593) *īʔā-* 'see' occurs in an independent clause, preceded by a clause with the switch reference marker.

(590) *gɨa eha-kɨ   īʔā Mandu pago   ērā ya   wiʔi-ge   siʔu*
 1x arrive-SR see Mandu mother 3p GEN house-LOC call

  bāhā-bõ
  goˆup-3fs
 Seeing that we had arrived, Mandu's mother went up and invited us to their house.

(591) ērā eropa ārī-kɨ pee-gɨ yɨʔɨ ērā-re ōpa ārī-bɨ
     3p thus say-SR hear-ms 1s 3p-SPC like^this say-NON3^PST
     Hearing them say that, I said like this to them...

(592) yɨʔɨ ōpa wa-ra-re yɨ pagɨ-sɨbārā pee-di-rā árī-bā
     1s like^this go-DVB-SPC 1s father-p hear-PST-ANp be-3p
     My parents heard (inferred) what happened to me.

(593) baha gahi-dō yɨʔɨ berā bāhā-rā ērā ii-kɨ ĩā-bɨ̃rĩ-bɨ
     a^lot other-CL 1s with PERT-ANp 3p do-SR see-HAB-NON3^PST
     I saw a lot of things (not good) that my friends did.

The verbs ārī- 'say' and ārī pepi- 'say, think' take quote complements embedded in the independent clause or as separate sentences. The quote clause is a propositional complement carrying an independent verb. In examples (594)–(595) it is bracketed:

(594) erop-ii-gɨ wāyõ-re daha [yɨ-re dos[27] árī-kɨ wā?gũ-ke]
     thus-do-ms aunt-SPC again [1s-SPC two be-SR wake^up-IMP]

     ārī-bɨ
     say-NON3^PST
     Then I said to my aunt, "Wake me at 2 a.m!"

(595) [yābīgā wa-rāka] pepi-a
     [tomorrow go-PROB^NON3^ANp] think-NON3^PRES
     I think we will go tomorrow.

However, the verbs were- 'say', weredīgī- 'talk', and weretabū- 'discuss' take as complements nominalized clauses functioning as the object of the main verb as shown in (596)–(597).

(596) ero-ge bāhā-rā ērā weredī-ra-re-ta were ii-bɨ ērā-re
     there-LOC PERT-ANp 3p talk-DVB-SPC-LIM say do-NON3^PST 3p-SPC
     We told them what those who live there had talked about.

(597) gɨa weredīgī-bɨ daha gɨa ii-ra-re, gɨa ii-bu-ri-re
     1x talk-NON3^PST again 1x do-DVB-SPC 1x do-POT-DVB-SPC
     We told again what we had done, and what we were going to do.

---

[27] Here dos 'two' is used as a loan word because Desano has no classifier for time of day.

Subordination

Verbs like *ābū-* 'to arrange/fix-up', *wia-* 'to give back', *boka-* 'find', *āī-* 'carry', *obeo-* 'send' take as object complement nominalized clauses such as (598)–(601).

(598) gɨa yẽ-ro   ii-ra-re   ābū   ii-bɨ   Maria bērā
      1x beˆbad-DVB do-DVB-SPC fixˆup do-NON3ˆPST Mary   with
      We made things right (lit., fixed up our bad-doing) with Mary's help.

(599) gɨa-re   ẽrā wayu-ra-re   árī-pe?re-ri-re
      1x-SPC 3p   lend-DVB-SPC be-TOTAL-DVB-SPC

      wia-pe?o-kā-bɨ
      deliver-TOTAL-ABS-NON3ˆPST
      We completely gave back everything they had lent us.

(600) yɨ?ɨ gābē-ri-sā-re   boka-pe?o-bɨ
      1s   want-DVB-also-SPC find-TOTAL-NON3ˆPST
      I found all I wanted.

(601) gɨa eha-bɨ   Villa Fatima-ge   ero   bāhā-rā   ẽrā
      1x   arrive-NON3ˆPST Villa Fatima-LOC there PERT-ANp 3p

      obeo-ri-re   āī-rā   eha-rā
      send-DVB-SPC carry-ANp arrive-ANp
      We arrived at Villa Fatima, arriving to carry what the people there were sending.

Nominalizations formed with the deverbalizer *-ro* may function as object complement of desiderative verbs. The verb root is either *gābē-* 'want' or a verb root plus the desiderative *-dia*. Examples (602)–(603) illustrate this form.

(602) bārī-re ẽrā gābē-ro   ii-rā   ii-bā
      1i-SPC   3p   want-DVB do-ANp do-3p
      They are doing to us as they want.

(603) ẽrā eha-dia-ro   eha-bā
      3p   arrive-DESID-DVB arrive-3p
      They arrived where they wanted to arrive.

Subject complements involve action nominalizations (604) or animate participant nominalizations as in (605)–(607).

(604) bɨʔɨ capitan árī-ri   dẽ   waha bārī-a
      2s   chief be-DVB first pay not^be-NON3^PRES
      Your being chief has always been worthless (from the beginning has been worthless).

(605) bāsɨ-re   paa-di-gɨ   duhara-bī
      man-SPC hit-PST-ms return-3ms
      The one who hit the man returned.

(606) õā-ro   bõʔbẽ-go   āʔrī-bõ
      be^good-DVB work-fs   be-3fs
      She is one who works well.

(607) Bogotá-ge   wa-bo-rã   õ-ge   doa-ke
      Bogotá-LOC go-POT-ANp here-LOC sit-IMP
      Those who are going to Bogotá sit here!

Nominalized forms functioning as constituents in noun phrases. It has already been noted that clauses functioning as the complement of other clauses may be viewed as headless relative clauses. The same is true of nominalized clauses that function as constituents in noun phrases. The same nominalizing suffixes are used, whether the nominalized clause functions as subject, direct object, indirect object, oblique object, possessor equative predicate of a predicate nominal, or noun phrase constituent.[28]

Nominalized clauses that modify a head noun are often in an appositive relationship with that noun. This is particularly clear when the head noun and nominalized clause are separated in the sentence, as in (608)–(609) (the nominalized clauses are bracketed).

(608) Alfonso era-bī   yābīka-ge   [Puerto Asis-ge   ari-di-gɨ]
      Alfonso arrive-3ms afternoon-LOC [Puerto Asis-LOC come-PST-ms]
      Alfonso, the one who came from Puerto Asis, arrived in the afternoon.

---

[28]Because the same problem is found in Barasano, Jones and Jones (1991:149) prefer not to use the term relative clause.

Subordination

(609) ērā kārēyā tĩʔrĩ-bā [gɨa ero-ge   api-di-rā]
     3p chicken hatch-3p [1x there-LOC place-PST-ANp]
     The chickens hatched, the ones that we had placed there.

In (610), not only are the head noun and nominalized clause separated in the sentence, but both have the specific object marker -re.

(610) karta-re   wia-bɨ   [ērā yɨ-re   Bītu-ge   obeo-ra-re]
     letter-SPC deliver-NON3^PST [3p 1s-SPC Mitu-LOC send-DVB-SPC]
     I delivered the letter, the one that they had sent from Mitu.

Even when the nominalized clause immediately follows the head noun, both may have a case marker, suggesting that they are still in an appositive relationship. In example (611), the locative marker -ge is attached to both the head noun and the nominalized clause.

(611) bākā-ge   [gɨa bāsā-ra   bākā-ge]
     town-LOC [1x grow^up-DVB town-LOC]
     the town where we grew up

In a few instances, however, the nominalized clause immediately follows the noun, and only the nominalized clause has a case marker. Such examples are best interpreted as headed relative clauses. In (612), for instance, the specific object marker -re is not attached to the head noun poga, but only to the nominalized clause that modifies it.

(612) poga   [ērā bē-ro   obeo-ra-re]   aĩ   era-bĩ
     manioc^cereal [3p little-n send-DVB-SPC] bring arrive-3ms
     He arrived bringing the bit of manioc cereal that they sent.

When a nominalized clause immediately follows a noun and neither has a case marker, it is unclear whether they should be interpreted as being in an appositive relationship or as a headed relative clause, for example, (613)–(614).

(613) yuhu-dɨ [lunes   árĩ-kɨ]
     one-day [Monday be-SR]
     One day, which was a Monday,...

(614) poga   [igo gari-ra]   bērā   suʔri-re   āsū-bõ
     manioc^cereal [3fs toast-DVB] with clothes-SPC buy-3fs
     She bought cloth with the manioc cereal she had toasted.

Nominalized verbs with -ri that appear before the noun, and that occur without arguments, are not considered relative clauses, but participial adjectives. They give a general rather than specific definition to the noun, as in example (615)

(615) kuri-ri   bāsā
      travel-DVB people
      traveling people

10.4–10.7 Adverbial clauses

Some adverbial functions are covered in the section on explicit medial clauses (§10.8). Besides those, there are adverbial clauses of time, manner, purpose, and location. Except for the purpose clause, they generally occur before the main verb. The time clauses tend to occur sentence initial as they often function as links to the preceding sentence. The location clauses occur anywhere in the sentence without any apparent change of meaning.

All of the adverbial clauses take either -ri or -ro (see §10.1), plus postpositions (§3.10) or other morphology. Unlike medial clauses they accept no aspectual or modal suffixes, but take the deverbalizer tense suffixes (see §10.1). One of the purpose clauses has the same subject as the main clause and takes one of the animate deverbalizers. This clause is included in this section, rather than §10.8, only for comparative purposes.

10.4. Time

There are time adverbial clauses that use postpositions to code 'before' and 'after', and a classifier to indicate 'while'.

Clauses that indicate that the main verb event occurs prior to the subordinate event are formed by a verb root, plus the potential marker -bo, plus the deverbalizing suffix -ro, followed by the postposition kore 'before', i.e., verb +bo +ro + kore.

(616) iri bākā bosedɨ wa-bo-ro   kore   árī-bɨ
      this town holiday go-POT-DVB before be-NON3^PST
      It was before the town holiday.

Clauses that indicate that the main verb event occurs following the subordinate event are formed by a verb root plus the past deverbalizing

Subordination

suffix *-ra* (*-ri* + *-a*) followed by the postposition *pɨʔrɨ* 'after', i.e., verb root + *-ra* + *pɨʔrɨ*.

(617) ba-tuʔa-ha-ra   pɨʔrɨ siete   árĩ-kɨ reunion ii-bɨ
      eat-COMPLET-TEL-DVB   after seven be-SR meeting do-NON3^PST
      After eating at seven, we had a meeting.

Clauses that express simultaneity with the independent clause are formed by a verb root, plus the deverbalizing suffix *-ri*, followed by the classifier *-subu* (§3.2) 'time', i.e., verb root + *-ri* + *-subu*.

(618) iri   eropa árĩ-ri-subu   yuhu conferencia wa-bɨ   daha
      this thus be-DVB-time   one conference go-NON3^PST   again
      While this was going on (lit., being), a conference happened again.

Besides the explicit clauses with the switch reference that refer to a certain time (see §10.8), there is another clause that expresses the meaning of 'at that time'. It is formed by a time word, plus the verb root *wa-* 'go', suffixed with *-ro*, followed by the accompaniment marker *bẽrã* (§4.3), i.e., verb root + *-ro* + *bẽrã*.

(619) ẽrã yãbɨka   wa-ro bẽrã bɨrĩ-a   ɨbã-ro-ge   kãrĩ-bã
      3p afternoon go-DVB with ascend-away high-DVB-LOC sleep-3p

      ẽrã
      3p
      In the late afternoon they climb up to a high place and sleep.

10.5. Manner

There are three types of adverbial clauses that express manner. The first has the meaning of 'do like' and consists of a verb root with or without the past marker *-di*, plus the deverbalizer *-ro*, plus the comparative postposition *dopa* 'like', i.e., verb ± *-di* + *-ro* + *dopa*.

(620) yɨʔɨ-sã ẽrã ii-di-ro   dopa-ta ii árĩ-ri-kɨ-a   yɨʔɨ
      1s-also 3p do-PST-DVB   like-LIM do be-DVB-VB-NON3^PRES   1s
      I also live/am like they were (ancestors).

The above construction can also describe a noun and consists of a noun, with or without *ii-ro* 'do-DVB', plus *dopa* 'like'.

(621) ïgɨ   ya   wiʔi   yaʔa   wiʔi   ii-ro   dopa   ã?ra-a
     3ms GEN house GEN^1s house do-DVB like be-NON3^PRES
     His house is like my house.

The second type has the meaning of 'without doing' and consists of a verb root, plus -ro, followed by the verb bārī- 'not be', plus -ro, i.e., verb + -ro + bārī- + -ro.

(622) gãbẽ   kẽã-ro   bārī-ro   kuri-ke   bɨʔɨ peyarã bērã
     RECIP fight-DVB not^be-DVB travel-IMP 2s   in-laws with
     Visit your in-laws without fighting!

The clause in (622) can also be formed by adding -ro to the negative passive construction (§6.2). The resulting form consists of a verb root, plus -ya, plus bārī- 'not^be', plus -ro.

(623) ba-ya   bārī-ro   ari-bɨ
     eat-PASS not^be-DVB come-NON3^PST
     We came without eating

The third type consists of the verb root, plus the deverbalizer -ri, plus the case marker bērã 'with', i.e., verb + -ri + bērã, and is often best translated by a simple adverb.

(624) erop-ii-rã   gɨa   õã-ro   būkūbiri-ri   bērã pepi-bɨ
     thus-do-ANp 1x   be^good-DVB be^happy-DVB with think-NON3^PST
     Therefore we thought very happily (lit., with happiness).

10.6. Purpose

There are three adverbial clauses of purpose. These usually follow the main verb.

The first clause has a different subject from the main verb. It consists of a verb root, plus -bo 'potential', plus -ro 'deverbalizer', with dopa 'like', i.e., verb + -bo + -ro + dopa as in (625). It may also occur with the negative marker as in (626).

(625) bɨã igo-re   karta   goha-bāsī-a   igo   bāsī-bo-ro   dopa-ta
     2p   3fs-SPC letter write-ABIL-NON3^PRES 3fs know-POT-DVB like-LIM
     You can write her a letter so that she will know.

Subordination

(626) *bari-re   bia   pūri-ri   eho-ke   ẽrã   wisi-biri-bo-ro   dopa*
food-SPC pepper hurt-DVB feed-IMP 3p hurt-NEG-POT-DVB like
Feed them food containing hot pepper so that they don't hurt (i.e., accustom them to the hot pepper)!

The second purpose clause has the same subject as the independent clause. It consists of a verb root, plus *-bo* (potential), plus one of the animate deverbalizers, i.e., verb + *-bo* + *-gɨ/-go/rã*. This clause is a post-final base of an explicit chain. The presence of *-bo* ensures that it is interpreted as a purpose clause.

(627) *wai   wẽhẽ-rã   wa-rã   ba-bo-rã*
fish kill-ANp go-HORT^IMP eat-POT-ANp
Let's go kill fish in order to eat!

The third purpose clause conveys the meaning of 'in order to do well'. It consists of a verb root, plus *-bã* (potential), plus *õã-ro* 'be^good-DVB', i.e., verb + *-bã* + *õã-ro*.

(628) *sã-bɨ   kãrẽyã   diu-ri-re   kãrẽyã   bãhɨ-rã   ẽrã*
put^in-NON3^PST chicken egg-p-SPC chicken child-ANp 3p

tɨʔrɨ-bã   õã-ro
hatch-POT be^good-DVB
We put the eggs in (the incubator) so that the baby chicks could hatch well.

The purpose clause can also occur in the negative as in (629), and when it does occur in the negative, it carries the same meaning as the purpose clause coded with a question (§8.1), as in (630).

(629) *õã-ro   wa-ke   bɨʔɨ dedere-biri-bã   õã-ro*
be^good-DVB go-IMP 2s be^lost-NEG-POT be^good-DVB
Go carefully so that you don't get lost!

(630) *õã-ro   wa-ke   bɨʔɨ dedere-ri   bɨ-ge*
be^good-DVB go-IMP 2s be^lost-Q 2s-LOC
Go carefully so that you don't get lost! (lit., (saying) "Will I get lost?")

The suffix *-bã* (potential) also occurs in the negative passive construction 'it is impossible' (see §6.2) to indicate what it is impossible to do.

(631) Gõábɨ buʔe-ri-re   kãʔbõtã-bã bãsɨ̃-ya
      God   teach-DVB-SPC block-POT be^able-PASS

   bãrĩ-k-a
   not^be-ASSUM-NON3^PRES
   It is impossible to block God's teaching.

Two clauses that close with the verb ãrĩ- 'say' function as purpose clauses. One clause consists of a verb root plus -poro (third person imperative) and the other with a verb root plus the question marker -ri (§8.1). In (630) above, the verb ãrĩ- 'say' does not follow the clause. In the majority of cases, however, it does as in (632).

(632) bɨrigã ɨi-ri   duha-biri-kã-poro   ãrĩ-rã   eropa-ii-bã
      much thick-DVB stay-NEG-ABS-IMP^3 say-ANp thus-do-3p
      In order that it not get too thick, they do like that.

10.7. Location

Adverbial clauses of location consist of the verb root with or without -bi 'negative' and -di 'past', plus -ro (deverbalizer) with or without -ge (locative), i.e., verb root ± -bi ± -di + -ro ± -ge.

(633) gahi-rã   yẽ-ro   ãrĩ weredɨ̃gɨ̃-bã gɨa pee-bi-ro-ge
      other-ANp be^bad-DVB say talk-3p   1x hear-NEG-DVB-LOC
      Others talked badly where we could not hear.

(634) bãrĩ árĩ-ro-ge   eha-rã   soo-bɨ
      1i   be-DVB-LOC arrive-ANp rest-NON3^PST
      On arriving at our place we rested.

(635) wiʔi árĩ-di-ro-ge   kãrĩ-yo-rã
      house be-PST-DVB-LOC sleep-HSY-3ANp
      They slept where a house had been.

10.8. Clause chaining and switch reference

As described by Longacre for Tucanoan languages (1985:278), Desano has two sorts of chaining structures, the implicit chain and the explicit chain, as regards the identification of participants. In the implicit chain, the same subject continues throughout the chain. In the explicit chain, overt markers indicate whether nonfinal clauses have the

Subordination

same or a different subject with reference to the main verb. The same-subject markers are the animate deverbalizers listed in §10.1.

Implicit chain. The implicit chain is a sentence structure which has essentially three parts: an initial link, a medial base which may occur several times, and a final base. It functions as a sequence sentence which encodes temporal succession.

The initial link, which may occur twice, consists of conjunctions and time statements such as 'after, one day', or adverbial clauses which recapitulate and refer back to a previous sentence as in (636)–(637).

(636) ērã eropa ii-kɨ gɨa bāsɨ-bɨ   pare
      3p thus   do-SR 1x know-NON3^PST finally
      When they did that, we finally understood.

(637) tuʔa-ha-dūgū   gasiru-re   tara-dēbō-bā
      finish-TEL-stand   canoe-SPC   drag-more-3p
      On finishing/having finished, they dragged the canoe some more.

The medial base has a simple or compound verb with no suffix, or with minimal aspectual and modal suffixes, including the negative marker as in (638).

(638) erop-ii-kɨ   ĩʔã yɨʔɨ sɨa-biri yɨʔɨ wiri-kā-bɨ   pare
      thus-do-SR see 1s   like-NEG 1s   leave-ABS-NON3^PST finally
      Seeing it was that way, I didn't like it and finally left.

Example (639) is a long implicit chain from a procedural discourse about making a canoe; the absence of a switch reference marker (see below) implies that the subject is the same throughout the sentence. One of the medial clauses has an embedded quotation followed by ārĩ- 'say'.

(639) tara-buʔa-ri   ōʔō iri-bā   bā   buʔa-ro-ge
      drag-descend-towards   here this-path path descend-DVB-LOC

      buʔara   tara-buʔa-ha   tara-bɨri-a   bārĩ
      descend drag-descend-TEL   drag-ascend-away^from   1i

      ārĩ-ro-ge   eha   tara-būhū-pi   ābū   sĩāĩ
      be-DVB-LOC   arrive drag-cause^ascend-place arrange plane

iripẽ-ta	*ōā-dia-a*		*ārĩ*	*pūrĩ*	*aĩ*	*waʔa*
no^more-LIM	be^good-DESID-NON3^PRES		say	leaves	carry	go

sẽo-ro   *gãʔbẽ-a*
open-n   want-NON3^PRES

Dragging (a hollowed-out log for a canoe) down here on this trail, we descend where the path descends (to the creek); dragging it down, then dragging it ascending, we arrive at our place. Dragging it up a little, we place (the canoe log) on the ground. Fixing it, we plane it then say, "No more; this will do." Then we go to bring leaves, as it is necessary now to open the canoe log (leaves are used to make the fire for opening the canoe).

In example (640), a nominalized clause is the complement of the medial verb *ĩʔã-* 'see'.

(640) *gɨa ya-re*   *ẽrã duri-sã-peʔo-kɨ*   *ĩʔã gɨa-re*
　　　1x GEN-SPC   3p load-put^into-TOTAL-SR   see 1x-SPC

　　　yãhã-dore-bĩ
　　　enter-command-3ms

Seeing that they finished loading our things (in the plane), he (the pilot) ordered us to get in.

The final base of the implicit medial chain has a regularly inflected verb as in (641).

(641) *iri*   *wiʔi-ge*   *eha*   *gahɨ-dõ-re-ta*   *weretabũ ii-bɨ*
　　　this   house-LOC   arrive   other-CL-SPC-LIM   discuss do-NON3^PST

On arriving at this house, we talked about other things (lit., talking did).

Explicit chain. Whereas implicit chains are sequence sentences that encode temporal succession between events of equal standing, medial bases in explicit chains usually encode background material for the foreground information expressed in the final and post-final base.

Explicit chains differ from implicit chains in that only one or two medial bases are usually found in an explicit chain. The events described in the medial and final clauses occur either concurrently or in temporal sequence, and a variety of relations between them may be deduced or marked: temporal setting (unmarked), conditional (unmarked),

Subordination

reason-result (unmarked), elaboration (unmarked), concession (marked by -*kere*), and contrafactuality (marked on the final base by the potential -*bu*). When a medial clause carries no marker, its primary relationship with the final clause of an explicit chain is usually background-foreground.

In narrative, medial clauses are commonly used to set a temporal setting for foreground events as in (642)–(644); note the use of -*kɨ̃* (switch reference) in some of these examples.

(642) ĩgɨ̃ po?ro eha-rã   ĩ?ã-bãrĩ-a   wa-kara-bɨ
      3ms   near   arrive-ANp see-not ͡be-PERF   go-seem-NON3 ͡PST
      When we arrived where he was, we were shocked.

(643) ĩgɨ̃ eropa ãrĩ-kɨ̃ yɨ-pɨ   ãrĩ-bɨ
      3s   thus   say-SR 1s-FOC say-NON3 ͡PST
      When he said that, I said...

(644) gɨa iri   bẽrã kóã-kɨ̃   dẽ   pe?re-biri-bɨ   deko
      1x   this with throw ͡away-SR first finish-NEG-NON3 ͡PST water
      When we threw it (water) out with this (pail), the water didn't even start drying up (i.e., we got nowhere near getting it all out of the hole).

A particularly common temporal setting involves the switch reference marker -*kɨ̃* and the verb *árĩ*- 'be' as in (645)–(646).

(645) soo-ri-dɨ̃   árĩ-kɨ̃-re
      rest-DVB-day be-SR-SPC
      on Sunday (lit., when it was the day for resting)

(646) cuatro árĩ-kɨ̃-ge du?u-bɨ̃ri-bɨ
      four   be-SR-LOC leave ͡off-HAB-NON3 ͡PST
      At four (each day) we stopped.

The medial clauses in the examples (647)–(648) may be interpreted as conditional margins.

(647) õã-ro   ĩbĩsĩ-a   baha   ii-kɨ̃
      be ͡good-DVB be ͡sweet-NON3 ͡PRES   a ͡lot do-SR
      If you do a lot, it is really sweet.

(648) ūba   ari-gɨ   ari-gɨkubī
doubt come-ms come-PROB^3ms
Who knows, if he comes, he comes.

The medial clause in example (649) may be thought of as providing the reason for the assertion of the final base.

(649) bĩā era-kɨ̃   ĩā-rā   gɨa bũkũbiri-a
2p   arrive-SR see-ANp 1x be^happy-NON3^PRES
Seeing that you arrived (because you arrived), we are happy.

A special clause that consists of a verb root nominalized by the deverbalizers *-ri* and *-ra* and followed by *dipuwaha* (head-pay) 'fault' or *waha* 'pay' produces a reason-result clause as in (650)–(651).

(650) gɨa bẽrẽ-ra   dipuwaha gɨa-re gɨa internado árī-ri-re
1x be^drunk-DVB fault   1x-SPC 1x dormitory be-DVB-SPC

biʔa-kā-bā
close-ABS-3p
Because of (lit., or the fault of) our getting drunk, they didn't allow us to be in the dormitory.

(651) yɨ bāgɨ-re bĩā ii-tabū-ri   waha Gōābɨ bĩā-re ōā-ro
1s son-SPC 2p do-help-DVB pay God   2p-SPC be^good-DVB

ii-kɨ̃   gāʔbẽ-a
do-SR want-NON3^PRES
Because of your helping my son (lit., for your helping my son pay), I want God to do good to you.

The concessive dependent clause is called a medial clause in the explicit chain because it takes the same form as the ones above with the addition of the suffix *-kere* (concessive) following the verb stem. It is followed by the explicit medial clause suffixes, and then usually the limiter marker *-ta*.

(652) ērā yɨ-re   eropa ārī-kere-kɨ-ta   yuhu-subu goru-re
      3p   1s-SPC thus   say-CONCES-SR-LIM   one-time   ball-SPC

   aku-bɨ
   put^in-NON3^PST
   Even though they said that, one time I made a basket.

The contrafactual sentence in Desano is a specialized version of the explicit chain. The medial clause is the same as other explicit chains; the final verb has the addition of the suffix -*bu* (potential marker) or -*bu* plus -*a* (recent past) giving the meaning of 'would have' as in (653).

(653) deko   bērē-biri-kɨ   ari-bua-yū-bā
      water fall-NEG-SR   come-CONTRAFACTUAL-ASSUM-3p
      If it hadn't rained, they would have come.

The final verb with -*bu* and without -*a* is the same as the least certain future (§5.3) shown in (654)–(655).

(654) ĩgɨ   ari-biri-kɨ   õā-buka
      3ms   come-NEG-SR   be^good-MIGHT^NON3
      It is better if he doesn't come.

(655) bɨʔɨ wa-kɨ   yɨʔɨ-sā   wa-buka
      2s   go-SR   1s-also   go-MIGHT^NON3
      If you were to go, I might go also.

Medial clauses with the same subject as the main verb are used not only to provide background information for the final base, but also to carry more information about the action described in the final base. In such instances, the final base typically has a verb of motion as in (656)–(657).

(656) iri-re   bāsī-gɨ   iri-re   bāsī-dia-gɨ   yɨʔɨ   ari-bɨ
      this-SPC   know-ms   this-SPC   know-DESID-ms   1s   come-NON3^PST
      I came wanting to know this (lit., to know this I came wanting to know this).

(657) gɨa waibɨrā   wēhē-rā   wa-bɨ
      1x   animals   kill-ANp   go-NON3^PST
      We went killing animals.

When a post-final base occurs instead of a medial one, the post-final base may or may not be in a background-foreground relationship with the final base. In example (658), for instance, the post-final base appears to give an important reason for the event expressed in the final base.

(658) *iri   conferencia gɨa bẽrã   árĩ-biri-bĩ   gua-gɨ*
      this   conference   1x   with   be-NEG-3ms   be^angry-ms
      He wasn't with us at this conference because he was angry (lit., being angry).

Similarly, in example (659), the additional information supplied in the post-final base appears to be the most important part of the sentence.

(659) *dẽ-re   ari-bɨ   yɨʔɨ õ-ge-re   SENA buʔe-gɨ*
      first-SPC come-NON3^PST 1s   here-LOC-SPC   SENA study-ms

      ari-gɨ
      come-ms
      First I came here (coming) to study SENA.

In contrast, the concessive post-final base in (660) appears only to supply background information. (See §10.4 for post-final bases with the potential marker *-bu/bo* which express the purpose of the final base.)

(660) *erop-ii-gɨ   yɨ-pɨ   bira-bira-bɨ   ẽrã   bẽrã árĩ-kere-gɨ-ta*
      thus-do-ms   1s-FOC   play-NEG-NON3^PST 3p   with be-CONCES-ms-LIM
      Therefore, I, for my part, did not play even though I was with them.

Explicit medial bases and implicit chain clauses can occur in the same sentence. In the example (661), for instance, the explicit medial base expresses the conditional ground 'if they don't soak the fruit' for the foreground information which is expressed in the implicit chain *oe sora-bã* 'they grate it and cook it'.

(661) *gahi-subu-re   wãsũpɨ-re   buʔu-bi-rã   oe   sora-bã*
      other-time-SPC   fruit-SPC   soak-NEG-ANp   grate   cook-3p
      Other times, if they don't soak the fruit, they grate it and cook it.

11
Pragmatic Considerations

Pragmatic matters discussed in this chapter are first, postpositional markers that constrain the way a sentence is processed with reference to its context, then the significance of constituent order variations, the introduction of referents, coherence devices, conjunctions, and episodic prominence. (The use of the auxiliary *ii-* 'do' as a backgrounding device is discussed in §5.9.)

11.1–11.3 Pragmatic markers

Three postpositional markers, which occur at the end of a noun phrase, indicate the ways in which a sentence is to be processed with reference to its context. They are contrastive *-pɨ*, additive *-sã*, and limiter *-ta* (with a more assertive form *-ta-bẽrã*). The markers *-pɨ*, *-sã*, and *-ta-bẽrã* precede the case marker *-re*, while *-ta* follows it.

11.1. The contrastive *-pɨ*

The presence of *-pɨ* in a sentence constrains the hearer to relate the constituent to which it is attached to a corresponding constituent of the context in a contrastive way. *-pɨ* can be attached to any noun phrase in the sentence, but most frequently occurs with the subject. With the subject it usually indicates that the new subject is going to carry out an action that is in contrast with that of the previous subject or was not expected.

(662) õã-ro   bira-ke   ārī-bɨ   yɨʔɨ yɨ bẽrã bãhã-rã-**pɨ**
      be^good-DVB play-IMP   say-NON3^PST 1s   1s with PERT-ANp-FOC

   yɨ-re   gahiropa   ārī   yɨʔri-bã
   1s-SPC otherwise say   answer-3p
   I said, "Play well!" (to my friends). They (in contrast) answered me otherwise.

(663) ārū-re   deko   bẽrã piu-bɨʔtã-bã   tuʔa-ha
      manioc^bread-SPC   water with pour-first-3p   finish-TEL

   yōkã   bẽrã piu   wãʔgū-bã   gahirã-**pɨ**
   manioc^juice   with pour raise^up-3p   others-FOC

   yōkã   diʔta piu-bã
   manioc^juice   only   pour-3p
   They first pour water in with the manioc bread. Then they pour in the manioc juice and stir it up. Others, in contrast, only pour in the manioc juice.

A related function of -*pɨ*, when attached to a subject as well as to an object, indirect object, or locative, is to show that the item so marked is in a contrastive relationship with a previously mentioned referent.

(664) yɨ-**pɨ**   wai-re   wẽhẽ-gɨ wa-bɨrī-bɨ
      1s-FOC   fish-SPC   kill-ms go-HAB-NON3^PST
      I (for my part) went fishing. (His brothers went to the field.)

(665) yave-ri-**pɨ**-re   dūgū-bã
      tap-p-FOC-SPC   place^standing-3p
      They put the taps in place (as opposed to the tubing talked about in the previous sentence).

(666) yɨ-**pɨ**-re   bari   o-bira-bã
      1s-FOC-SPC   food   give-NEG-3p
      They didn't give food to me. (They did to others.)

(667) bākã-**pɨ**   bõʔbẽ-bɨ
      town-FOC   work-NON3^PST
      I worked in a town (as compared to working before in the jungle).

11.2. The additive -sã

The marker -sã 'also' occurs with any noun phrase in the sentence. The presence of -sã constrains the hearer to relate the constituent to which it is attached to a corresponding constituent of the context in an additive way.

(668) ẽrã monseñor comisario-**sã**-re   ãrĩ-bã
      3p bishop   commissioner-also-SPC said-3p
      They spoke to the bishop and the commissioner also.

Between sentences, -sã indicates that a different subject is going to do the same action as the one mentioned previously, and a different object and location are going to receive the same action as in (669)–(670). (This is opposed to -pɨ where the action would be different.) Example (670) shows the relative order of -ge 'locative', -sã , and -re.

(669) ĩgɨ-**sã**   kãrĩ oya-bĩ
      3ms-also sleep lie-3ms
      (Like the other animals mentioned) he also lies down to sleep.

(670) doʔpa-ge-**sã**-re   gũyã-rãka
      now-LOC-also-SPC think-PROB^NON3^ANp
      We will think also at this time (as we thought before about our friends).

There are a few instances of -pɨ and -sã occurring in the same noun phrase. In example (671) it appears that the speaker wanted to contrast the subjects because there was an antagonistic relationship between the two speakers, but also show that they were talking in the same way to one another.

(671) Lino-**pɨ-sã**   eropa-ta ãrĩ-bĩ   ĩgɨ-re
      Lino-FOC-also thus-LIM say-3ms 3ms-SPC
      Lino, for his part, also said to him (talked in the same manner).

11.3. The limiters -ta and ta-bẽrã

The marker -ta in Desano is a limiter with glosses 'exactly, precisely, just'. It may be attached to any clause constituent except the independent verb, although occasionally it follows an independent verb when it is in the imperative form, as in (672).

(672) ari-ke-*ta*
come-IMP-LIM
Okay, come!

Its pragmatic effects vary with the constituent and the context, but are basically twofold. Technically, the presence of -*ta* constrains the constituent to which it is attached to be either (1) identified with or (2) limited to some corresponding constituent of the context. The first effect is the most productive.

The sameness constraint, i.e., when information is reiterated, the presence of -*ta* may constrain the constituent (or the whole assertion) to which it is attached to be identified with the previous mention of the constituent (or assertion). This is illustrated in examples (673)–(676); -*ta* frequently occurs with the concessive adverbial clause because the concessive clause either states or implies reiterated information as in (677).

(673) *suʔri   koe-go   ii-ri   suʔri   koe-go-ta   ii-a*
clothes wash-fs do-Q clothes wash-fs-LIM do-NON3^PRES
Are you washing clothes? Exactly, I am washing clothes.

(674) *ero-ge-ta   eha-bã*
there-LOC-LIM arrive-3p
They arrived right there (at the place mentioned earlier in the discourse).

(675) *gɨa conferencia peʔo-ri-dɨ-ta   wa-bĩ*
1x   conference finish-DVB-day-LIM go-3ms
He went on the very day our conference finished.

(676) *yābɨka-re-ta   era-bã*
afternoon-SPC-LIM arrive-3p
They arrived that same afternoon.

(677) *ẽrã bẽrã árɨ-kere-gɨ-ta*
3p   with be-CONCES-ms-LIM
Even though (I) was with them,...

Pragmatic Considerations

The limiting constraint is shown by the presence of -ta to constrain the hearer to limit the reference of the constituent concerned to the referent stated and no other as in (678)–(679). In a question, the presence of -ta constrains the addressee to indicate whether the reference of the constituent to which it is attached is to be limited to the stated referent as in (680).

(678) gasi-ri bẽrã-**ta**   sora-bã
 bark-p with-LIM cook-3p
 They cook it with bark (not with anything else).

(679) cuatro-dɨ-ri-**ta** ã?rĩ yɨ?ɨ ari-bɨ   pare
 four-day-p-LIM be 1s come-NON3^PST finally
 (After) being (there) for just four days I finally came.

(680) bɨ̃ã pe-rã-**ta**   a?ri-ri
 2p two-ANp-LIM come-Q
 Did just the two of you come?

There are several grammaticalized expressions in Desano of which -ta forms a part such as those in (681)–(682).

(681) ii-bu-bẽhẽ-**ta**
 do-POT-NEG-LIM
 but (see §11.7)

(682) iri-pẽ-**ta**
 this-CL-LIM
 That's it!

The marker -ta-bẽrã (LIM-with) 'in particular' is a stronger limiter than -ta alone and is used less frequently. Whereas -ta follows -re, -ta-bẽrã precedes it.

(683) iri-subu-**ta-bẽrã**-re   wa-biri-kã-rã   ãrĩ-bɨ   gɨa
 this-time-LIM-with-SPC go-NEG-ABS-HORT say-NON3^PST 1x
 "Let's not go at this particular time!" we said.

(684) õã   dõbẽ-**ta-bẽrã**   tebo-ri-kɨ-bã
 these women-LIM-with suffer-DVB-VB-3p
 Women in particular are the ones who suffer.

11.4. Pragmatic considerations affecting constituent order

Studies in Desano have shown that SOV is the most common constituent order and that oblique expressions occur twice as often before the verb as after. Usually, the order of dependent clauses within the sentence reflects the relative order of events represented by the respective clauses. Thus, the implicit medial clauses (§10.8) always occur before the verb, as in example (685), as do explicit medial conditional clauses (686), whereas purpose clauses usually occur following the verb, as in (687). A locative goal (688) will often follow the verb because in a certain sense it corresponds to the sequence of events (the goal is reached only when the event described in the verb is completed).

(685) wēhẽ duhara ba?a árĩ-rãka
   kill return eat be-PROB^NON3^ANp
   We hunt, return, and eat.

(686) deko bērẽ-kɨ wa-sobẽ yɨ?ɨ
   water fall-SR go-FUT^NEG 1s
   If it rains I will not go.

(687) wai wēhẽ-rã wa-rã ba-bo-rã
   fish kill-ANp go-HORT eat-POT-ANp
   Let's go catch fish in order to eat!

(688) bu?a-bɨ   Finca Bonaire-ge
   go^down-NON3^PST farm Bonaire-LOC
   (We) went down to the Bonaire farm.

Variations from the SOV order can be explained under the following two parameters. (1) Fronting to provide thematic coherence at points of disunity, plus explicit medial clauses functioning as a link (see §11.7).[29] Under this parameter would be time words, such as *pɨ?rɨ* 'afterwards', *iribohegere* 'a long time ago'; subordinate clauses such as *erop-ii-kɨ* 'do thus'; demonstrative pronouns; and other pronouns that refer to a previously mentioned noun, such as the anaphoric pronoun *iri* 'this/that'. (2) Supportive, non-salient, amplificatory, appositive information follows the verb.
   Examples (689)–(690) are two portions of text that illustrate these two parameters. To the right of the phrase or clause being illustrated is

---

[29] This would be termed topicality according to Dik (1981:4–74).

the number of the parameter which it illustrates. (The introduction of participants is discussed in §11.6.) The examples of parameter 2 in these two portions illustrate appositive or amplificatory information following the verb.

(689) gɨa iri-re ba?a ii-bɨ   [usual word order]
      1x this-SPC eat do-NON3^PST

   iri-re [1] gɨa ba-ri-subu   era-bā   kubeo bāhā-rā pe-rā [2]
   this-SPC 1x eat-DVB-time arrive-3p Cubeo PERT-ANp two-ANp

   gɨa [1] ērā era-kɨ   ĩ?ā [1] ērā-re bokatīrī-bɨ
   1x   3p arrive-SR see   3p-SPC greet-NON3^PST
   We ate this. While we were eating this, two Cubeo people arrived. We seeing them arrive, greeted them.

(690) erop-ii-rā gɨa [1] Gōābɨ ya-re   bu?e-rā gɨa ya bērā
      thus-do-ANp 1x   God   GEN-SPC study-ANp 1x GEN with

   bu?e-a   wīrā   ya bērā [2] i-re [1] gɨa-re si?u
   study-NON3^PRES Desano GEN with   this-SPC 1x-SPC call

   bu?e-rā   katekista ā?rī-bā Gōābɨ ya-re   si?u bu?e-rā [2]
   teach-ANp catechist be-3p   God   GEN-SPC call teach-ANp
   Therefore, we, when we study God's Word, study in our language, in Desano. Those who call us together to teach us this are catechists, the ones who call us together to teach us God's Word.

Parameter 2 is also illustrated in the fact that the subject and indirect object generally precede the quote verb ārī- 'say' when it opens the quote, but they always follow ārī- at quote closure because it is repeated, known information.

(691) yɨ?ɨ ērā-re ōpa   ārī-bɨ   "..." ārī-bɨ   yɨ-pɨ
      1s   3p-SPC like^this say-NON3^PST "..." say-NON3^PST 1s-FOC

      ērā-re
      3p-SPC
   I said thusly to them "...," said I to them.

Stories are sometimes introduced by the time words *dē-* 'at the beginning', *iribohe-ge* 'a long time ago', and *kore-ge* 'before time'. These time words are most often fronted since the beginning of a text is a point of discontinuity.

(692) *dē-ge-re   yɨʔɨ   bābɨ̄   árī-dɨgā-gɨ*
     first-LOC-SPC 1s   young^man be-begin-ms
     At the beginning, when I was newly a young man,...

(693) *dē-re   ari-bɨ   yɨʔɨ*
     first-SPC come-NON3^PST 1s
     At the beginning I came.

(694) *iri-bohe-ge-re   yɨʔɨ bāhī-gɨ   árī-kɨ̄ ge-re*
     this-time-LOC-SPC 1s child-ms be-SR-LOC-SPC
     A long time ago, when I was a child,...

In example (695), however, the subject (introduced with *yuhu-* 'one' §11.6) is topical, rather than the time word, which therefore follows the verb.

(695) *yuhu-go dōbēo   árī-bɨ̄rī-po   kore-ge-re*
     one-fs   woman   be-HAB-HSY^3fs   before-LOC-SPC
     There was a woman a long time ago.

11.5. Introduction of participants

The existential verb *árī-* 'be' is used to tell what the text is going to be about, as in a text on ticks in (696)–(697).

(696) *ɨ̄gɨ̄ wekɨ   tēhē   árī-yū-bī*
     3ms danta tick   be-ASSUM-3ms
     There was a danta tick.

(697) *tēhē-a árī-yū-bā*
     tick-p be-ASSUM-3p
     There were ticks.

In (696), the tick is also introduced with the pronoun *ɨ̄gɨ̄* 'he', whereas in (697) there is no definite pronoun because in the same text the speaker switches from talking about specific ticks to just talking about them in a general way so that they then become referential but not definite.

Participants are frequently introduced with *yuhu-* 'one' which seems to mean 'a certain' to indicate that that referent is a definite person or thing, although probably not known to the listener previously, and that it is going to be salient in the discourse. See examples (695) and (698)–(699).

(698) *yuhu conferencia wa-bɨ*
 one conference go-NON3^PST
 A conference took place.

(699) *yuhu-go bɨro Victoria wãĩ-kɨ-go poʔro waʔa*
 one-fs lady Victoria name-VB-fs near go
 On going to where a lady named Victoria was,...

The text can be introduced by a sentence naming the participants and the action about which the story revolves.[30]

(700) *yuhu-dɨ gɨa wapikɨ-rã waibɨrã wẽhẽ-rã wa-bɨ*
 one-day 1x four-ANp animals kill-ANp go-NON3^PST
 One day, we four went hunting (names were also given).

Some differences have been noted between the introduction of salient and nonsalient participants in a text. In some cases the word *gahi-* 'other' is used along with the name of the nonsalient participant, as in (701):

(701) *profesore gahi-rã yẽ-ro weredɨgɨ-bã*
 professor other-ANp be^bad-DVB talk-3p
 Others, professors, talked bad (about us).

Most frequently nonsalient participants are not named. Rather, the use of a third person plural marker implies their presence.

(702) *ĩgɨ-re Bĩtu-ge aĩ-gã-bã*
 3ms-SPC Mitu-LOC carry-MOVE-3p
 They took him to Mitu.

---

[30] The use of *yuhu-* in the expression *yuhu-dɨ* 'one day' implies that the day is salient in the discourse in the sense that salient events occurred on that day.

(703) peru ïi-bo-rã   kï-re   baha dua-bã
beer do-POT-ANp manioc-SPC a^lot pull^out-3p
When they are about to make beer, they harvest a lot of manioc.

Two examples of introduction of participants from the same text are given in (704)–(705). In (704) the participants are named after the final verb. In (705), they are named before. Although the subject usually precedes the verb, in sentences with 'presentational articulation' (Andrews 1985:77–80) in which a participant is introduced to a story with a verb like 'arrive', it is common in many languages for the reference to the participant to follow the verb; in Spanish, for example, *llegaron dos cubeos* 'arrived two Cubeos'.

(704) iri-re   gɨa ba-ri-subu   era-bã   kubeo bãhã-rã   pe-rã
this-SPC 1x eat-DVB-time arrive-3p Cubeo PERT-ANp two-ANp
While we were eating this, two Cubeo people arrived.

(705) yuhu-gɨ bɨrẽagɨ   bẽrã bãrãpo bãgɨ era-bã
one-ms Carapana with wife child arrive-3p
A Carapana man with his wife and child arrived.

11.6. Coherence devices

Thematic coherence is mentioned in §11.5. The theme of the text or event line is connected throughout the text by means of the connectors discussed below. The absence of a connecting device signals that there is a break in action continuity, and that the sentence provides amplification, a speaker comment, or a summing up of the preceding information, rather than proceding to the next event. Example (706) shows amplification in the second sentence.

(706) gɨa peru i?ri-bɨ   gɨa õã-ro   i?ri-bɨ
1x beer drink-NON3^PST 1x be^good-DVB drink-NON3^PST
We drank beer. We drank it well (without problems).

The connecting devices always occur at the beginning of the sentence. Five types are discussed. They are the initial link for the implicit and the explicit chain (§10.8).

The first type is a productive connecting device which is further reference to the last event using lexical overlap with the previous verb repeated in a subordinate clause, with or without *eropa* 'thus'. The events so linked are in a coordinative relationship. It can also be an implied reference to that event with the verb *tuʔa-ha-dūgū* 'finish-TEL-stand'. Many of these clauses are the time adverbial clauses discussed in §10.4. Note examples (707)–(709).

(707) *buʔa-ra-bɨ*   *buʔa-ra*
      go^down-towards-NON3^PST go^down-towards
      (We) went down. On going down,...

(708) *eropa weredīgī-tuʔa-ha baʔa-bɨ*
      thus   talk-COMPLET-TEL eat-NON3^PST
      On finishing talking like that, we ate.

(709) *tuʔaha-dūgū Tomasu gɨa-re sērēpi-bī*
      finish-stand Thomas 1x-SPC ask-3ms
      On finishing that, Thomas asked us.

Secondly, time words also act as connectors as in (710)–(712).

(710) *pɨʔrɨ wāʔgā ii-bɨ*
      after get^up do-NON3^PST
      Later we got up.

(711) *iʔre-dɨ̄   pɨʔrɨ koʔro-bā kībo-re*
      three-day after peel-3p   fermented^manioc-SPC
      After three days they peel the fermented manioc root.

(712) *gahi-dɨ̄   Arsenio Lomalinda-ge   duha   wa-bī*
      other-day Arsenio Lomalinda-LOC return go-3ms
      The next day Arsenio returned to Lomalinda.

Thirdly, the demonstrative *iri* 'this/that' (an anaphoric pronoun) and the location pronoun *ero* 'there' also provide coherence in the discourse as shown in (713)–(714).

(713) *iri-pa-ge   bihi-bā*
      this-CL-LOC strain-3p
      They strain it into this (dish).

(714) *ero-ge   árī-gɨ buʔe-bɨ*
      there-LOC be-ms study-NON3^PST
      While being there I studied.

Fourthly, maintaining coherence while changing subjects in an episode can be accomplished by the use of unmarked or marked participles of the verbs *pee-* 'hear' or *ĩʔã-* 'see' following a tail-head linkage construction, i.e., repetition of the verb stem from the previous sentence with a switch reference marker. This type of subordinate clause is described in §10.1. The form *eropa* 'thus' occurs very frequently with this construction.

(715) ãrĩ-bĩ   ĩgɨ   eropa ãrĩ-kɨ   pee
      say-3ms 3ms   thus   say-SR   hear
      He said. On hearing him say like that, (she)...

(716) yukɨ dɨpɨ-ge   peya-bĩ   ĩgɨ eropa peya-kɨ   ĩã-gɨ
      tree branch-LOC   beˆperched-3ms   3ms thus beˆperched-SR   see-ms
      He perched on the branch. On seeing that he was perched there, (I)...

Finally, the grammaticalized adverbial clause *erop-ii-* plus a same subject marker (thus-do-ms/fs/ANp/n) protypically functions as a logical connector meaning 'therefore' or as a conclusion statement as in (717); this clause often serves to link large chunks of the discourse. For example, in a folktale, following a paragraph talking about what some animal women did, a paragraph discussing what the opossum did is introduced as in (720); and these two connecting devices can be combined as in (719)–(720).

(717) erop-ii-gɨ   dɨgɨ-ge   kuri-gɨ   ĩã-ro   gãʔbẽ-a
      thus-do-ms   jungle-LOC   travel-ms   see-n   want-NON3ˆPRES
      Therefore, when traveling in the jungle, look carefully (there are snakes)!

(718) eropa-ii   oa-pɨ   bẽgã so-gɨ   waʔa wa-pɨ
      thus-do   opossum-FOC   ants get-ms   go   go-HSYˆ3ms
      In the meantime, the opossum went off gathering ants.

(719) ero-re   gɨa buʔe-ri-subu-re-ta   dõbẽ-sã   buʔe-bã
      there-SPC 1x   study-DVB-time-SPC-LIM   women-also   study-3p
      The same time we studied there, the women also studied.

(720) eropa ii-ra   pɨʔrɨ
      thus do-DVB after
      After doing that,...

Pragmatic Considerations

In the following narrative text, the connecting devices and pragmatic markers are bracketed.

(721) (a) [iribohe-ge-re   yɨʔɨ bāhī-gɨ árī-kɨ-ge-re]   yɨʔɨ pagɨ
       [longˆago-LOC-SPC 1s   child-ms be-SR-LOC-SPC] 1s   father

          pɨʔrɨ bāhā-rā   baya-bɨrī-bā
          after PERT-ANp dance-HAB-3p

    (b) [eropa baya-rā]   buya-kɨ-bɨrī-bā
       [thus   dance-ANp] necklace-VB-HAB-3p

    (c) [tuʔa-ha]   dōbē-[pɨ]   gūrūyā   ērā-re sū-bɨrī-bā
       [finish-TEL] women-[FOC] prepare 3p-SPC paint-HAB-3p

    (d) [eropa sū-rā]   kabā-kɨ-rā   ii-a   ārī-bā
       [thus   paint-ANp] relationship-VB-ANp do-NON3ˆPRES say-3p

    (e) yɨʔɨ-[pɨ] [ērā erop-ii-kɨ]   īā-gɨ   gūyā-bɨrī-bɨ
       1s-[FOC] [3p thus-DO-SR] see-ms think-HAB-NON3ˆPST

    (f) yɨʔɨ[-sā] ērā iro dopa-ta ii-dia-ri-k-a
       1s-[also] 3p do like-LIM do-DESID-FRUST-ASSUM-NON3ˆPRES

          ārī pepi-bɨrī-bɨ
          say think-HAB-NON3ˆPST

    (g) [erop-ii-gɨ]   [doʔpa-ge-re]   yɨ pagɨ   sīri-ra   pɨʔrɨ-ge
       [thus-do-ms] [still-LOC-SPC] 1s father die-DVB after-LOC

          yɨʔɨ[-sā] ērā ii-di-ro   dopa-ta   ii-a
          1s-[also] 3p do-PST-DVB like-LIM do-NON3ˆPRES

    (h) yɨ pagɨ-sɨbārā bērā ōā-ri-re   bɨā-re were-a
       1s father-p   with beˆgood-DVB-SPC 2p-SPC say-NON3ˆPRES

    (i) iri-pē-ta   āʔrā-a
       this-CL-LIM be-NON3ˆPRES

(a) [A long time ago, when I was a child,] my father and his relatives (lit., those after father) customarily danced. (b) [When they danced like that,] they adorned themselves with necklaces. (c) [At that,] the ladies, [for their part], prepared cosmetics and painted their bodies and faces. (d) [On painting them,] they said, "We are in a brother relationship with them." (e) I, [for my part], [seeing them do like that,] thought a lot. (f) "I [also] want to do like they do," I thought. (g) [Therefore,] [at this time,] since my father has died, being older, I [also,] do like they used to do. (h) I am telling you about the good things with my father. (i) This is it.

In the above text, sentence (a) begins with two introducers, 'long ago, when I was a child', both marked with *-re* to establish the frame for this short text. Sentence (b) has the connecting device that reiterates the previous verb and, by means of a same subject marker, shows that the final verb will have the same subject. Sentence (c) begins with the connecting device *tuʔaha*, then the presence of *-pɨ* constrains 'the ladies' to be contrasted with a corresponding constituent in the context, viz 'my father and relatives'. Sentence (d) begins with the same connecting device as sentence (b), which implies a coordinative relationship with sentence (c). In sentence (e), the change of topic is signalled in two ways: by *-pɨ* on the first person singular pronoun which is fronted for prominence, and by the connecting device 'thus-do-with switch reference' that provides continuity while changing participants. Within the thought expressed in sentence (f), *sã* occurring with the first person singular pronoun constrains that referent to be added to a corresponding constituent who performed the same action(s). On sentence (g), *eropiigɨ* introduces a logical conclusion to the body of the discourse, with *doʔpagere* 'now' setting the time frame for the conclusion. *-sã* attached to the first person singular pronoun, however, indicates that the action he does is similar to the previous actions performed by the previous participants. The absence of a connecting device in sentence (h) indicates a discontinuity and, in fact, sentence (h) is not part of the event line. The speaker was making a comment summing up the discourse. Finally, sentence (i) is a closure sentence frequently used in Desano discourse.

11.7. Conjunctions

Apart from *erop-ii-* plus a same subject marker (discussed in §11.6), two phrases in Desano function as conjunctions.

The conjunction *ii-bu-bẽhẽ-ta* 'but' (§11.3) occurs sentence initially and acts as a conjunction between two sentences to show that what is expected to occur in the second sentence is not happening. It is illustrated in (722) but is not frequently used.

(722) yɨʔɨ buʔe-ri-sã   õã-pũrĩ-k-a
      1s   study-DVB-also be^good-INTEN-ASSUM-NON3^PRES

      ii-bu-bẽhẽ-ta   yɨ-re gahi-dõ bãrĩ-a
      do-POT-NEG-LIM 1s-SPC other-CL not^be-NON3^PRES
      My studies are also very good, but I don't have anything.

The second conjunction in Desano is *eropa árĩ-kɨ* (thus be-SR). It can occur sentence intitially as in (723) or within the sentence as part of a list with the meaning 'and' as in (724).

(723) eropa árĩ-kɨ ẽrã-sã ari-biri-bã
      thus be-SR 3p-also come-NEG-3p
      And they also didn't come.

(724) ari-bɨ   Rita bẽrã Mandu bẽrã Mandu eropa árĩ-kɨ
      come-NON3^PST Rita with Mandu with Mandu thus be-SR

      Kerebẽte
      Clement
      I came with Rita, Mandu, Mandu, and Clement.

11.8. Episodic prominence

The particle *pare* has the meaning of 'finally' or 'in the end'. It is used to mark the resolution of a problem, the completion of a goal, or the conclusion of a series of actions. In one text that tells about harmony in a village, it occurs on the sentences that tell about the breaking of that harmony. In that case, and often in the discourse, *pare* coincides with a climactic point and usually occurs more than once in that sentence. Example (725) illustrates *daha* funtioning at the sentence level to mean 'again'.

(725) ii-ke   daha
      do-IMP again
      Do it again!

In a narrative, *daha* is often found on sentences preceding the climax to indicate that these statements are leading up to the goal or conclusion but have not yet reached it. In a text telling about going from his village to another location for a course, the speaker has various climactic points coded with *pare*, with *daha* usually found in the preceding sentences. In one case he tells about the first ones arriving at a course location, and then the people arriving over the next few days. He uses *daha* when telling about getting up the first day when they were there by themselves. He then uses it to tell about the arrival of some other students that were from near their own location (726); he then tells about others coming in (727), without using *daha*, then uses *pare* in (728) when everyone has arrived and when classes start.

(726) pɨʔrɨ daha iri yābɨka-re-ta   daha era-bā Aka bāhā-rā
after again this afternoon-SPC-LIM again arrive-3p Aca PERT-ANp
Later (again), in the afternoon (again) people from Aca arrived.

(727) erop-ii-rā   pare gahi-pɨ-ri bāhā-rā-sā   era-peʔre-kā-bā
thus-do-ANp finally other-CL-p PERT-ANp-also arrive-TOTAL-ABS-3p

   pare
   finally
Therefore, finally, those from other locations also completely arrived (everyone arrived).

(728) iri pɨʔrɨ pare yuhu-dɨ̃ lunes   árɨ̃-kɨ̃ klase dɨ̃gā-bɨ
this after finally one-day Monday be-SR class begin-NON3^PST

   pare
   finally
After this, finally, on Monday classes finally began.

References

Andrews, A. 1985. The major functions of the noun phrase. In T. Shopen (ed.), Language typology and syntactic description 1, 62–154. Cambridge: Cambridge University Press.

Barnes, Janet. 1990. Classifiers in Tuyuca. In David L. Payne (ed.), Amazonian linguistics, 273–92. Austin: University of Texas Press.

———. 1996. Autosegments with three-way lexical contrasts in Tuyuca. International Journal of American Linguistics 62(1):31–58.

Bivin, William Edward. 1986. The nasal harmonies of twelve South American languages. M.A. thesis. University of Texas at Arlington.

Comrie, Bernard. 1985. Causative verb formation and other verb-driving morphology. In T. Shopen (ed.), Language typology and syntactic description 3: Grammatical categories and the lexicon, 309–48. Cambridge: Cambridge University Press.

Dik, Simon. 1981. On the typology of focus phenomena. In Jeun Hoekstra, Harry Van de Hulst, and Michael Moortgat (eds.), Perspectives on functional grammar, 4–74. Dordrecht: Foris Publications.

Dixon, Robert M. W. 1982. Where have all the adjectives gone? and other essays in semantics and syntax. Janua Linguarum Series Maior 107. Amsterdam: Mouton Publishers.

Fillmore, Charles J. 1975. Santa Cruz lectures on deixis, 1971. Bloomington: Indiana University Press.

Givón, Talmy. 1990. Syntax: A functional typological introduction, 2. Amsterdam: John Benjamins.

Haiman, John. 1983. Iconic and economic motivations. Language 59:781–819.

Hopper, Paul and Sandra Thompson. 1984. The discourse basis for lexical categories in universal grammar. Language 60(4):703–52.

Jones, Wendell and Paula Jones. 1991. Barasano syntax. Studies in the languages of Colombia 2, Summer Institute of Linguistics and the University of Texas at Arlington Publications in Linguistics 101. Dallas.

Kaye, Jonathan Derek. 1970. The Desano verb: Problems in semantics, syntax, and phonology. Ph.D. dissertation. Columbia University.

———. 1971. Nasal harmony in Desano. Linguistic Inquiry 2:37–56.

Keenan, E. 1985. Relative clauses. In T. Shopen (ed.), Language typology and syntactic description 2: Complex constructions, 141–70. Cambridge: Cambridge University Press.

Longacre, Robert. 1985. Sentences as combinations of clauses. In T. Shopen (ed.), Language typology and syntactic description 2: Complex constructions, 235–86. Cambridge: Cambridge University Press.

Macauley, Monica. 1993. Reduplication and the structure of the Karuk verb stem. International Journal of American Linguistics 59(1):64–81.

Malone, Terrell. 1982. Focus in Tuyuca. ms.

———. 1991. Proto Tucanoan and Tucanoan genetic relationships. ms.

Miller, Marion. 1976. Sistemas fonológicos de idiomas colombianos, Tomo 3, Fonología del desano, 105–12. Lomalinda, Meta, Colombia: Editorial Townsend.

———. To appear. Diccionario desano-español.

Palmer, F. R. 1986. Mood and modality. Cambridge Textbooks in Linguistics. Cambridge: Cambridge University Press.

Payne, Thomas E. 1992. Field manual for descriptive linguistics. ms.

Waltz, Nathan and Alva Wheeler. 1972. Proto-Tucanoan. In Esther Matteson (ed)., Comparative studies in Amerindian languages. Janua Linguarum 127:119–49. Mouton: The Hague.

www.ingramcontent.com/pod-product-compliance
Lightning Source LLC
Chambersburg PA
CBHW070331230426
43663CB00011B/2275